Hamilton Boy

BISHOP AND PRESBYTERY

Bishop and Presbytery
THE CHURCH OF SCOTLAND
1661–1688

by

Walter Roland Foster

St. Andrew's Theological Seminary
Manila

PUBLISHED FOR THE CHURCH HISTORICAL SOCIETY

LONDON
S · P · C · K
1958

First published in 1958
by S.P.C.K.
Holy Trinity Church
Marylebone Road
London, N.W.1.

Made and printed in Great Britain by
Spottiswoode, Ballantyne and Co., Ltd.
London and Colchester

To

ROBERT S. BOSHER

AUTHOR'S NOTE

It is somewhat presumptuous for an American who has never visited Scotland to write about one period of the ecclesiastical history of that distinguished land. That it is possible to do so at all is due primarily to the numerous historical clubs which flourished in Scotland in the last century as well as to-day. The wealth of journals, records, diaries, and other documents which have been so painstakingly prepared and printed have placed all students of Scottish history in their debt. My own dependence upon the labours of these clubs is sufficiently evident in the pages which follow.

Much has been written about the period of the "Second Episcopacy". Too frequently, however, the dramatic character of the struggle between the Establishment and the Covenanters has dominated the history of these years. The records of the period suggest that another development of at least equal significance was taking place, namely the partial integration of presbyterianism and episcopacy. It was a development which probably has been unknown in the history of the Church in any other land and which represents a significant chapter in the heritage of the Church of Scotland.

I wish to acknowledge the help I have received from many persons in the preparation of this book. I am especially conscious of all that I owe to Dr Robert S. Bosher. His interest and direction have been unceasing and the criticism and advice which he has given have helped at every stage of preparation. I wish to thank the Dean of St Andrew's Theological Seminary in Manila, the Right Reverend Norman S. Binsted, the Dean of the General Theological Seminary, and the Overseas Department of the American Episcopal Church for making it possible for me to spend the time on this study and for much other assistance; Dr Powel Mills Dawley who read the manuscript and made numerous valuable suggestions; the library staff of the General Theological Seminary for their willing and efficient help on many occasions; Mrs John Talbot who typed the manuscript; Mr Dean Calcote who checked references; and my wife who read the manuscript. The publication of *A Profest Papist: Bishop John Gordon*, by T. F. Taylor, has brought to light much new information about that controversial figure and I have been able to read the proofs of the pamphlet through the courtesy of S.P.C.K.

WALTER ROLAND FOSTER

ACKNOWLEDGEMENTS

Thanks are due to the following for permission to include copyright material:

The Clarendon Press (Gilbert Burnet: *History of My Own Time*).

Hodder and Stoughton Ltd. (G. D. Henderson: *The Claims of the Church of Scotland*; D. Butler: *The Life and Letters of Robert Leighton*).

Morehouse-Gorham Co. Inc. (Arthur Lowndes: *Vindication of Anglican Orders*).

Thomas Nelson and Sons Ltd. (W. C. Dickinson and G. Donaldson: *A Source Book of Scottish History*).

Scottish History Society (William Mackay (Ed.): *The Chronicles of the Frasers*, 916–1674).

The Third Spalding Club (G. D. Henderson and H. H. Porter (Eds.): *James Gordon's Diary* 1692–1710).

CONTENTS

1

THE HISTORY OF THE KIRK: 1661-1688

THE restoration of Charles II in May 1660 was celebrated in Scotland with the same spontaneous rejoicing that greeted the returned monarch in England. John Nicoll wrote that at Edinburgh

> a great number of the citizens, went to the Mercat Croce of Edinburgh, quahir a great long boord . . . wes coverd with all soirtes of sweit meittis, and thair drank the Kinges helth, and his brether; the spoutes of the Croce rynnand all that tyme with abundance of clareyt wyne. . . . And in the meantyme . . . the haill bellis in Edinburgh and Cannongait did reign, the drumes did beatt, trumpettis sounded. . . . Farder, at nycht thair was bonefyres put out throw the haill streitis of Edinburgh, and fyre workis both thair and at the Castell of Edinburgh . . . till eftir xij hours and moir.[1]

The popularity with which the new reign began was indicative of a dramatic change in the loyalties and affections of the people of Scotland. During the Interregnum, the alliance of Presbyterians with the nobility, which alone made it possible for the nation to wage war with Charles I, had been fatally broken by internal divisions within Presbyterianism itself. Dissension within Scotland and the defeat at Worcester led to almost a decade of English rule, enforced by an English army of occupation. It was a subjection deeply resented in Scotland. For that nation, the restoration of the ancient royal line meant release from foreign domination. The rebellion of the past was decisively repudiated in the popular wave of enthusiasm which greeted the re-establishment of royal authority.

However, this reaction was not only political in character,

[1] John Nicoll, *A Diary of Publick Transactions and other occurrences chiefly in Scotland*, p. 293.

but had religious implications as well. The conflicts of the Interregnum had meant the discrediting of Presbyterianism for many. Robert Douglas, one of the important presbyterian leaders, wrote in 1660 that "there is now a generation risen up, which have never been acquainted with the work of reformation . . . you will not believe what a heart-hatred they bear to the covenant".[1] Three weeks later he wrote that "whatever church government be settled there [in England], it will have an influence on this kingdom; for the generality of this new upstart generation have no love to Presbyterial government but are wearied of that yoke, feeding themselves with the fancy of Episcopacy, or moderate Episcopacy".[2] For such people the restoration of the royal line symbolized that of the whole of civil and religious life as it had been known in the first part of the seventeenth century.

Most important was the change which had taken place in the nobility. Disillusioned by the internal dissension within Presbyterianism and resentful of the interference of the Kirk in matters of government, the younger nobility had come to the conclusion that Presbyterianism was foreign to the spirit and traditions of a feudal nobility. Episcopacy was part of the old order which they were anxious to restore. The ecclesiastical policy of Charles II would never have been possible without their support.

Understandably enough, the presbyterian leaders in Scotland were alarmed about the nature of the approaching religious settlement. Their envoy to the royal court, James Sharp, returned in August 1660 with a letter from Charles in which he promised that "We do . . . resolve to protect and preserve the government of the Church of Scotland, as it is settled by law, without violation".[3] The letter allayed some suspicion, which is probably just what it was designed to do.

However, the actions of the new Parliament in 1661 were far from reassuring. Subscription to the Solemn League and Covenant was quietly ignored, and on 28 March the Act Rescissory was passed which repealed all Acts of Parliament since 1640. This Act

---

[1] Robert Wodrow, *The History of the Sufferings of the Church of Scotland*, 1, 16.
[2] Ibid., p. 21.   [3] Ibid., p. 81.

at least made it an open question as to what that ecclesiastical government was which was "settled by law".

No Act of Parliament and no royal promise or resolution could alter the fact that Scotland was deeply divided in its religious affections. The presbyterian party itself was split between the Resolutioners, who were in the majority, and the intense and determined Protestors. A third party rejected any presbyterian settlement and supported at least a moderate episcopacy. Douglas testified to the existence of these three groups in his correspondence with Sharp.

There are three parties here, who have all of them their own fears in this great crisis; the protestors fear that the king come in; those above mentioned [those favouring episcopacy] that if he come in upon covenant terms, they be disappointed; and those who love religion and the liberty of the nation [the Resolutioners] that if he come not in upon the terms of the league and covenant, his coming in will be disadvantageous to religion and the liberty of the three nations.[1]

At the time there were many reasons which may have led Charles to believe that an episcopal settlement would be as acceptable to Scotland as it had been in the days of James VI, and that it was the best solution of a difficult problem. There could be no question about meeting the demands of the Protestors. The Resolutioners also had lost the support of the nobility, and it was believed that there was considerable sentiment for episcopacy. Finally, Charles could never be accused of insincerity when he wrote of the "unsuitableness thereof to our monarchical estate [of that] church-government, as it hath been exercised these twenty-three years past".[2]

The whole political and ecclesiastical trend was to re-establish the pattern of government known in the days of James VI. The operation of the Privy Council (a portion of which sat in London, as in the days of James VI), the method of election of the members of the new Parliament, and the whole tenor of government clearly

---

[1] Wodrow, *History*, I, 16–17.
[2] Thomas Stephen, *The History of the Church of Scotland*, II, 443.

showed this trend. It can hardly have been much of a surprise
when the Privy Council in Scotland received a letter from Charles,
dated 14 August 1661, which ordered the restoration of that "right
government by bishops".[1] The letter was received on 5 September and the decision proclaimed throughout Scotland. On
14 November a writ passed the great seal nominating Dr James
Sharp to the metropolitan see of St Andrews. On 15 December
James Sharp, Andrew Fairfowl, Robert Leighton, and James
Hamilton were consecrated in London; on 2 January 1662 a
royal letter forbade the presbyterian courts to meet without episcopal approval. On 7 May six prelates were consecrated in Edinburgh and on the following day were restored to their place in
Parliament to "represent the first state".[2] On 27 May an Act was
passed for the "Restitution and Re-establishment of the ancient
Government of the Church by Archbishops and Bishops . . . as
the church government most agreeable to the Word of God, most
convenient and effectuall for the preservation of treuth, order and
unitie and most suteable to monarchie and the peace and quyet of
the state".[3] The bishops were restored "to the exercise of their
episcopall function, presidencie in the church, power of ordination,
inflicting of censures and all other acts of church discipline". On
11 June an Act was passed requiring all who had taken possession
of a benefice since 1649, when patronage was suppressed, to secure
presentation and collation from the bishop.[4] Acts were passed
condemning covenants against the King and forbidding "diverse
unlawfull meitings and conventicles".[5] Beginning in October 1662
diocesan synods were held throughout the country, and until 1688
kirk-sessions, presbyteries, and diocesan synods met regularly.
Although an Act for the establishment of a National Synod was
passed in 1663, it did not convene during the Restoration period.

A large number of Protestors were not willing to conform to the
settlement and accept collation from a bishop. By February 1663
most of these had been ejected from their parishes. Those who

[1] Stephen, *History*, II, 443.
[2] *Source Book of Scottish History*, III, 156.
[3] Ibid., p. 157.   [4] Ibid., pp. 162–4.   [5] Ibid., pp. 158–9.

favoured an episcopal settlement, as well as a large majority of the Resolutioners, did conform. The number of nonconforming clergy is still a matter of debate, but probably between 250 and 300 out of a total of 900 refused to conform. Nonconformity was concentrated in the south-west.

Much of the subsequent history of the Church of Scotland is a story of alternate attempts to repress or indulge the covenanting clergy. Archbishop Leighton in 1674 referred to the struggles in the south-west as a "drunken scuffle in the dark",[1] and went on:

> . . . we have still been tossed betwixt the opposite extreams of too great rigour and too great relaxations and indulgences, well made lawes too severe to be executed & for a counterpoise have executed almost none of them, except by exorbitant fitts and starts.[2]

From 1662 until 1667 a general attempt was made to enforce conformity by Parliament and the Privy Council. Conventicles were forbidden by Act of Parliament in 1662; the "Mile Act" of August 1663 forbade deprived ministers to reside within twenty miles of their former cure, and in 1663 fines were imposed upon all who "wilfully . . . absent themselffs from the ordinary meitings of divine worship in their oune paroche church on the Lord's day".[3] At the suggestion of Archbishop Sharp, the Court of High Commission was revived; however, it had little success and was suppressed within a few years. This policy of repression, which was parallel to the contemporary policy in England, was administered mainly by the Earl of Rothes and Archbishop Sharp.

The policy was opposed by John Maitland, Earl of Lauderdale and Secretary for Scotland in London, who was destined to become the most powerful man in Scotland. The Pentland Rising in November 1666 also helped to discredit the policy. It was believed by the Government that nonconforming clergy had played a large part in instigating the rebellion.[4] Although the rebellion

---

[1] *Lauderdale Papers*, III, 76.
[2] Historical MSS. Commission *Eleventh Report*, Appendix, part vi: The MSS. of the Duke of Hamilton, K.T., pp. 148–9. Quoted in Butler, *Life and Letters of Robert Leighton*, p. 476.
[3] *Source Book of Scottish History*, III, 165.
[4] *Lauderdale Papers*, I, 254.

was a small one and apparently unplanned, still the Government
was nervous and the memory of the late troubles remained un-
dimmed. Lauderdale was convinced that repression only incited
the Covenanters to rebellion and that a policy of conciliation and
indulgence was preferable. The Pentland Rising seemed to prove
his point, and Charles agreed.

By the end of 1667 the new policy was well under way. A large
part of the army was disbanded in August 1667, and in October
of that year an amnesty was declared for those involved in the late
rebellion. The First Royal Indulgence was issued on 7 June 1669,
which offered manse, glebe, and a minimal stipend to nonconforming clergy who would abide "peaceably and orderly" in their
parishes and not intrude on neighbouring parishes. About forty
ministers, mostly in the Diocese of Glasgow, accepted the indulgence. Lauderdale himself became Royal Commissioner in that
year, and in 1670 Bishop Leighton began discussions on his Accommodation Scheme with six leading nonconformist clergy. This was
an unsuccessful attempt to comprehend all dissenters by expanding
the terms of the settlement.[1] On 3 September 1672 a Second
Indulgence was issued by the Privy Council to all clergy "outed
since the year 1661 . . . permitting and allowing them to preach
and exercise the other pairtes of the ministeriall function in
the paroches to which they are . . . confyned by this present
act".[2] About forty-five Nonconformists took advantage of this
indulgence.

The policy of conciliation was not a successful one. Nonconformist activity was encouraged by the absence of persecution, and
field conventicles grew in number and size until by 1670 there was
practically a schismatic Church in the south-west. Thus in 1670,
in the midst of discussions on the Accommodation Scheme, the
Government passed one of its most severe Acts against nonconformity—the so-called "Clanking Act". This Act, which was
renewed two years later, imposed heavy fines on all who held
house conventicles, and ordered that all "shall be punished with

---

[1] See below, pp. 28 ff.
[2] *Source Book of Scottish History*, III, 168.

death . . . [who] preach, expound scripture or pray at any . . . feild conventicle".[1] Fortunately, the Act was not enforced.

A third phase of the period, characterized by renewed repression, lasted from 1674 until 1679. Archbishop Leighton retired to England, and Alexander Burnet, who had been deprived of the see of Glasgow in 1670 for opposing the indulgence policy, was restored in September of 1674. In December he was readmitted to the Privy Council. A royal proclamation "obliging Heritors and Masters to keep their dependents from Conventicles"[2] was issued on 18 June 1674 and reissued in 1677. On 6 August 1675 Charles issued Letters of Intercommuning forbidding all contact with certain specified rebels. In 1678 the so-called Highland Host was recruited from the Highlands and quartered on the southwest for about six weeks or two months. During these years, the conventicles took on a more specifically military character, and the murder of Archbishop James Sharp of St Andrews on 3 May 1679 was followed at the end of the month by the second insurrection of the Covenanters. This was a considerably larger rebellion than the one of 1666. An armed conventicle defeated the government forces under Graham of Claverhouse on 1 June, but the rebels themselves were decisively crushed at Bothwell Brig by the Duke of Monmouth on 22 June 1679. Most of the prisoners were allowed to return home, although a small number were sent to Barbados only to perish by shipwreck in Orkney on the way. One week after the defeat at Bothwell Brig, Charles issued a Third Indulgence permitting house conventicles, suspending fines for conventicles, and permitting all to preach who would give "surety . . . to our privy councill for their peaceable behaviour, only one preacher being allowed to a parish".[3]

The defeat of 1679 brought submission or at least acquiescence from most Nonconformists for the remainder of the reign. The period from 1680 to 1685 is marked mostly by a few minor and radical movements which are somewhat reminiscent of similar movements during the Interregnum in England. The "Sweet Singers", a radical, sectarian group, were imprisoned in 1681;

[1] *Source Book of Scottish History*, III, 172.   [2] Ibid.   [3] Ibid., p. 174.

B

while the Cameronians, who claimed to be "the contending and suffering remnant of the true Presbyterians of the Church of Scotland",[1] saw their leaders, Richard Cameron and Donald Cargill, successively killed or captured and executed. These radical movements attracted almost no support from the moderate Nonconformists and only succeeded in drawing a good deal of unjust persecution upon the south-west in 1682–3.

Repressive measures were also taken throughout the entire period against Quakers and Roman Catholics. However, these two groups were unorganized and attracted few adherents; they were never as serious a threat to the Establishment as the nonconformity of the south-west.[2]

Meanwhile the terms of the settlement itself had been further elucidated by three important Acts of Parliament. In 1662 the National Covenant and the Solemn League and Covenant were declared to be "in themselffs unlawfull oaths and . . . against the fundamentall lawes and liberties"[3] of the subjects of the kingdom. In October 1669 the Assertory Act defined the relationship between Crown and Church. The moderate language of the Act of 1661, which spoke of the monarch as "supreme governor of this kingdom over all persons and in all causes", was altered to declare that "his Majestie hath the Supream Authority and Supremacie over all persons and in all causes ecclesiasticall within this kingdom".[4] The bishops of Scotland were soon to discover that the Act was far from being a mere formality. The Act shows clearly the kind of royal absolutism under which the Scottish Church laboured, and which was the greatest burden of the Church. Every attempt which churchmen made to modify this absolutism or to take any independent action was doomed to failure. In a country where any interference by the Government

[1] *Source Book of Scottish History*, III, 182.

[2] For the extent of Quakerism, see "The Quaker Movement in Scotland", by John Torrance, *Records of the Scottish Church History Society*, v, 31 ff. Also Henderson, *Religious Life in Seventeenth-Century Scotland*, c, x. For Roman Catholicism, see "Roman Catholicism in Scotland in the Reign of Charles II", by Prof. Donald Maclean, *Records of the Scottish Church History Society*, v, 43 ff.

[3] *Source Book of Scottish History*, III, 159.   [4] Ibid., 160.

in the affairs of the Church was called Erastianism, the royal supremacy expressed by the Assertory Act made it extraordinarily difficult for the Restoration Church to commend itself to the "generality of the people".[1]

The Test Act, passed on 31 August 1681, was a further indication of the extent of royal authority over the Church. The Test, imposed on a wide variety of civil and ecclesiastical authorities, required subscription to the Scots Confession of 1560. Although only moderately Calvinistic, the Confession was quite unacceptable to clergy of the Aberdeen school. The Bishop of Aberdeen also pointed out that it was difficult to reconcile the Scots Confession with that recognition of royal supremacy which the Test required. Several other internal inconsistencies, such as the promise to maintain the existing Church settlement along with an acknowledgment of the royal right to alter it, as well as the specific recognition of the Duke of York's right to the succession, made the oath unacceptable to many. It was only after the Government explained away both the inconsistencies and the Scots Confession that most of the clergy took the Test. Even so, about eighty clergy refused and were deprived.[2]

Upon the accession of James VII the strength of loyalty to the royal cause was amply demonstrated by the rapidity with which the rebellion of the Earl of Argyll was suppressed in June 1685. The Earl himself was captured and executed. However, royal authority was not able to enforce as drastic a change in the religious settlement as James desired. His proposals for toleration of the "Roman Catholick religion" aroused the Scottish Parliament in June 1686 to their first rejection of royal policy in the entire Restoration period. On 21 August 1686 a royal letter was issued granting Romanists free private exercise of their religion. In the following year two royal indulgences were issued, the second of which permitted all religious meetings except field conventicles.

The Second Indulgence was accepted by most of the non-conforming clergy except the Cameronians, and in July 1687 an

---

[1] See below, p. 10.
[2] Gilbert Burnet, *History of My Own Time*, II, 318.

address of thanks to His Majesty was drawn up by the indulged clergy in Edinburgh. However, a large segment of opinion was probably well expressed by the students of the University of Edinburgh, who in 1680 and again in 1681 carried an effigy of the Pope up Blackfriars' Wynd to the High Street. "The figure was clothed in a calico gown, and sat in a chair. Having set it down on the street, they set fire to it, causing a quantity of powder within the body to explode and burst it all in pieces." [1]

Scotland played little active part in the Revolution of 1688–9. Nevertheless, the Roman policy of James had alienated large parts of the kingdom, and the events which took place in England were welcomed by many in Scotland. A Scottish Convention was summoned by William III and it met on 14 March 1689. The Whig leader, the Duke of Hamilton, was chosen president by a majority of fifteen votes. After the Jacobite minority had withdrawn, the Whig rump declared that James had forfeited the crown by his violation of the laws of the kingdom. They adopted a Claim of Right, modelled on the English Bill of Rights. One article of the Claim declared that "Prelacy . . . hath been a great and insupportable grievance and trouble to this Nation, and contrary to the inclinations of the generality of the people".[2] It was further ordered that William and Mary should be proclaimed and prayed for as king and queen. Since the bishops of the Church of Scotland were nonjuring, the King agreed to abolish episcopal government, and in 1689 an Act abolishing Prelacy was passed by Parliament. On 7 June 1690 an Act establishing presbyterian government brought the Restoration settlement to its final end.

The involved and dramatic history of the Covenanters during the entire period has sometimes tended to obscure the fact that, for the most part, they could count on the active allegiance of only a small minority of the population and were largely confined to one area of Scotland. There was, it is true, considerable discontent with royal policy. The loss of free trade with England, the economically disastrous war with Holland, and arbitrary government

---

[1] *Domestic Annals of Scotland*, II, 413.
[2] *Source Book of Scottish History*, III, 205.

by a few favoured individuals, all served to discredit royal authority. Yet, until the issue of popery was raised by James VII, there was never any question of solving these problems by rebellion. That method had been tried before, and the nation was not anxious to resort to it again. The insurrections of the Covenanters failed to secure support among the nobility or to attract many of the common people.

While in the south-west there was a good deal of popular unrest and, at best, unwilling submission, the ordinary Scotsman north of the Tay seems to have been quite content with the Restoration Church. Indeed, his loyalty to an episcopal settlement was to be amply demonstrated after the Revolution. In the south-east the settlement was, at least, tolerable to the majority of the people. It must be remembered that the average parishioner would see very little change in his kirk. Except in nonconformist areas, he would see the same minister, and the ordinary worship and discipline of the kirk was largely unchanged. In large areas of Scotland which were troubled only slightly by nonconformity, the Restoration Church was making an attempt to combine presbyterian and episcopal elements into one religious settlement—an attempt which has too often been ignored and which, in the long run, may prove to be of even more interest and import than the "Sufferings of the Church of Scotland".

2

THE SPIRITUAL AND FIRST ESTATE

ON Tuesday, the eighth day of April, 1662, "the Archbischop of St Androis, the Archebischope of Glasgow, and the Bischop of Galloway, being upone thair jurnet toward Scotland . . . a great number of the nobilitie, barones, gentillmen, burgessis, in and about Edinburgh, raid out to meit thame . . . and with all reverence and respect resauit and imbraced thame in great pomp and grandour, with sound of trumpet, and all uther courteseis requisite".[1] Thus did a contemporary describe the arrival of three of the four bishops who had been newly consecrated in London the previous December. It is worth noting that the most distinguished prelate of them all, Robert Leighton, the saintly Bishop of Dunblane, had separated himself from the other three and quietly slipped into Edinburgh. Nor did he take any part in the great services or processions of the following month.

On 22 January 1662 Charles II sent a letter to his Royal Commissioner, the Earl of Middleton, with instructions concerning the status of bishops:

> His Matie being firmlie resolved that the honour authoritie and dignitie of his three estates of Parliament in his kingdome of Scotland, according to the ancient and fundamentall constitution thereof, shall be restored and maintained in their integretie, without any alteration or diminition, yow are to take caire that the estate of Bishops as the spirituall and first estate be restored at the nixt session of our Parlt . . . [and] that the Archbishops and Bishops be restored to ther ancient and accustomed dignities privileges and jurisdictions, especiallie the jurisdiction of Comissariots and receaving of the coattes of testaments . . . [and moreover] that the

[1] Nicoll, pp. 363-4.

Bishops presented by us may have ther clame right and possession for the year 1661 and all years following to whatsoever wes possest or might have beine possest legallie be ther predicesso's.[1]

The faithful Scottish Parliament was not slow to obey the royal command. On 7 May six new bishops were consecrated at Edinburgh by Sharp, Fairfowl, and Hamilton. On the following day the assembled prelates were solemnly escorted to Parliament,

> . . . being convoyit fra the Archebischop of Sant Androis hous with 2 erles . . . and the 2 Archebischops in the midst betuix the 2 Erles, besyde much uther companyes of the Provest, bailleis, and counsell of Edinburgh, with barones, gentillmen, and utheris in great number. The haill Bischops come to the Parliament all in thair gownis . . .[2]

Not only was there little real opposition in Parliament to the restoration of bishops, but also there were a number of signs that the restoration was welcomed by many. More than a year earlier, when some Church leaders were still hoping for a presbyterian settlement, James Sharp had written from Edinburgh that ". . . if the Church government [now Presbyterian] did depend upon the vote of this Parliament it would undoubtedly be overturned",[3] and again the next month he wrote that ". . . I am confident were it putt the vote within ten dayes presbytrie would doun & episcopacy set up".[4]

James Sharp's predictions were correct, and throughout the Restoration the fourteen bishops of Scotland were to take their place in every Parliament. Robert S. Rait, in his important book, *The Parliaments of Scotland*, suggests that there were two reasons why bishops were restored: (1) in the ancient constitution they represented the first estate, and it was fit at this time to return to the ancient structure, and (2) they were still technically landowners who actually claimed in 1685 to be the "King's barons". Thus their presence was consistent with a Scottish Parliament which tended to be composed of those who represented the land.[5]

---

[1] *Lauderdale Papers*, I, 296–7.   [2] Nicoll, p. 366.
[3] *Lauderdale Papers*, I, 72.   [4] Ibid., p. 80.
[5] Rait, *Parliaments of Scotland*, p. 176. For the lands of the bishops, see below, p. 34.

Bishops were expected to attend Parliament whenever it met and were fined for absences. In 1662 it was enacted that prelates absent from Parliament after 27 May 1662 "without a lawfull excuse tymely represented and admitted" should be fined 1200*l.* *Scots.* They were liable to a fine of 12*l.* *Scots* for each day's absence without leave, and 6*l.* *Scots* if they took their seats after the calling of the roll.[1]

Only one member of the bench, Robert Leighton, seems deliberately to have refused this duty. Always sensitive to anything which would offend Nonconformists, he avoided Parliament except when religious matters were being discussed. In 1662 he announced before Parliament that although he had taken the Oath of Allegiance and Supremacy, he did not take it as a Member of Parliament. He added: "Neither had I been here today, were it not that I understood you were to be about Church affairs, and that which concerns ministers."[2]

Numerically the bishops represented a small percentage of Parliament. At best there could be but fourteen bishops, and the average attendance at Parliament, which sat as one house, was around 150. These figures, however, give a very misleading impression of the strength of the episcopal vote, for the bishops' influence was much greater than their numbers would indicate. The Scottish Parliament, like the Church of Scotland, was very different from its English counterpart. While there was some growth of parliamentary opposition throughout the period, for the most part Parliament was almost entirely subservient to royal control, especially during the reign of Charles II. Much of this control was exercised through a group known as the Committee of the Articles, and in this Committee the bishops had a crucial position. The Committee of the Articles was used by Charles II, as it had been used by James VI, as an effective instrument for the control of Parliament. No measure could be introduced save that which the Articles presented, and Parliament was called upon

---

[1] *Acts of Parliament*, VII, 371–2.
[2] Blair, *Life*, p. 409. Quoted in Butler, *Life and Letters of Robert Leighton*, p. 347. See also Burnet, *History*, I, 253.

simply to approve or reject that which was presented to it. Not only did the bishops comprise about one-fourth of this Committee, but they had also a major voice in the election of all other members. Charles II revived the method of election used by James VI. The method was well illustrated in 1663 when

> . . . the clergie retired to the Exchequer Chamber and the nobility to the Innerhouse of the Session (the barrons and burgesses keeping their place in the Parliament House). The clergie made choise of eight noblemen to be on the Articles . . . and the nobilitie made choise of eight bishops . . . which being done the clergie and nobilitie met together in the inner Excheckquer house, and, haveing shoune their elections to other, the persons elected, at least so many of them as were present, stayed together in that room (whilst all others removed) and they jointly made choise of eight barrones and eight commissioners of burrowes . . . and then represented the whole elections to His Maiesties Commissioner. [1]

With such a method of election, it is clear that the vote of the bishops determined the character of the nobility's membership on this important committee, and that between them the character of all other members was decided. Since there could be no question about the royal control of the episcopate, it was a scheme ideally suited to the royal control of Parliament.

It is not surprising to find that in 1674 Charles severely reprimanded three Scottish nobles who "endeavor'd to undermine the very foundation of his authority, by offering to bring in things in plain Parliament, without bringing them first to the Articles; which Articles he lookt upon as the securest fence of his government".[2] Nor is it surprising that the Convention of 1689, called by William III, presented in its Articles of Grievances as its first complaint "that the committee of parliament called the Articles is a great greivance to the nation, and that there ought to be no committees of parliament but such as are freely chosen by the estates to prepare motions and overtures that are first made in the house".[3] William III's efforts to retain even a severely reformed

---

[1] *Source Book of Scottish History*, III, 239–40.
[2] Ibid., p. 253.   [3] Ibid., p. 207.

Committee of the Articles were unsuccessful, and on 8 May 1690 "Our soverayne lord and lady the king and queens majesties, with advyce and consent of the estates of parliament, doe heirby discharge and abrogate in all tyme comeing the forsaid committee of parliament called the Articles".[1]

The place of the bishops in Parliament and on the Committee of the Articles makes it clear that they held an important place within the legislative branch of the government of Scotland. While their duties here would take them away from the work of their dioceses, the demands upon their time were by no means as heavy as upon English bishops. Parliament did not meet regularly, and there were long periods when it did not meet at all. No Parliament was held from 1663 until 1669, and again none met between 1674 and 1681. Yet there are some signs that the absence of the bishop from his diocese when Parliament did meet had its effect upon the Church. On 12 June 1672 the Presbytery of Elgin ordered that "the Lord Bischop being to repair to the South to the Parliament, it is ordained that the brethren per vices supplie his absence by preaching one the Tuysdayes in Elgin untill he returne".[2] On 7 October 1675 the Synod of Aberdeen noted that there have been "three vacand Synods then preceeding, which were not keeped whilst the Bishop was at Edinburgh",[3] presumably attending the meetings of Parliament then in session. On 4 May 1686 the Synod of Ross noted that it did not "keep its last intended meeting because the Bishop went to attend the Parliament".[4]

In addition to their duties in Parliament, bishops had important duties in the executive and judicial branches of the Government. The two Archbishops of St Andrews and Glasgow were members of the Privy Council. Since the Privy Council had great responsibilities, especially during the long intervals when Parliament

---

[1] *Source Book of Scottish History*, III, p. 240. For the whole subject of the Articles, see Rait, *The Parliaments of Scotland*, pp. 367–91.
[2] *Records of Elgin*, II, 374.
[3] *Records of the Meeting of the Exercise of Alford*, pp. 252–3.
[4] *Records of the Presbyteries of Inverness and Dingwall*, p. 363.

did not meet, a large amount of the time and efforts of the two archbishops were required by this body.

Other bishops also were assigned civil responsibilities in the Government. Thus in the first years of the new reign, George Wishart was a member of a committee on taxation, a commission for the universities, and the Commission for the Planting of Kirks and Valuation of Teinds.[1] The practice continued throughout the period. Andrew Bruce, Bishop of Dunkeld, attended the Parliament of 1685 and was appointed a Lord of the Articles, a Commissioner for Trade, and a member of the Commission for the Plantation of Kirks and Valuation of Teinds.[2]

One of the important civil responsibilities of the bishops was their supervision of the Commissary Courts. These courts were really descendants of the pre-Reformation Ecclesiastical Courts and were revived by Act of Parliament in 1609. In 1662 the bishops were restored to their jurisdiction of commissariots according to the Act of 1609, which was ratified and renewed. The courts were more or less synonymous with the dioceses, and the commissioners and their deputies were appointed by the bishop. When a bishop was consecrated, it was customary for Parliament to ratify specifically his commissariot jurisdiction. Thus David Fletcher was consecrated Bishop of Argyll on 3 June 1662, and on 9 September of that year Parliament passed a "Ratification in favor of David Bishop of Argyll of the jurisdiction of Commissariotship within the dyocie of Argyll".[3] The Commissary Courts were set up for confirmation of wills and decision of divorce and slander causes. They had jurisdiction in small debt cases and were Courts of Record.[4] Moreover, they were given jurisdiction "in all spirituall and ecclesiasticall couses controvertit betwene ony persones dwelling within the boundis and dioceses of thair prelaceis and bischoprickes." [5] Four commissaries, two appointed by each archbishop, were to dwell in Edinburgh, to have sole

[1] "Montrose's Chaplain", *Records of the Scottish Church History Society*, v, 46.
[2] Hunter, *The Diocese and Presbytery of Dunkeld*, I, 220
[3] *Acts of Parliament*, VII, 433.
[4] Thomson, *Public Records of Scotland*, pp. 115–16.
[5] *Source Book of Scottish History*, III, 59.

jurisdiction over divorce cases and to act as a Court of Appeal from the other commissaries. The Lords of Session were in turn a Court of Appeal from their decision.

The right to appoint the commissaries, the commissaries-deputy, the commissary clerks, the commissary-clerks-deputy, and the procurator-fiscals was in the hands of the bishop, but his choice was sometimes influenced by non-ecclesiastical factors. In 1673 Robert Leighton, Archbishop of Glasgow, wrote to the Lord Commissioner, the Duke of Lauderdale, to apologize for an appointment which he had made:

> The Comissariate of Lanrick becoming vacant I was forc't to dispatch ye choyce of one for it on purpose to avoyd the crowds of severall recomendations, and ye vexatious importunities with wch they were press'd. Ye person I have chosen is one John Graham, Comissary Clerk of Dunblain, & have putt another in his place there, being under some kind of promise to the both to doe them a kindnes . . . but that which pains mee now most in this particular is yt I understand by ye Earle of Kincardin that yor grace had a mind to recomend one to yt place, wch could I have had ye least foresight of, there is no doubt it would have bin reserv'd for him.

Leighton hoped that the Duke would understand, but

> yet after all this rather then yor grace should take it ill. . . . I would doe my utmost & I hope might prevayl with my freind to surrender back his gift; but if yor grace incline not to putt him & mee to ye retrograde I would engate myself for ye gentleman for whom yor grace design'd this place that ye first & best of that kind within ye diocese, if it fall vacant in my time, should be no otherwise disposed of.[1]

A few of the appointments were hardly worthy ones. On 18 October 1682 Andrew Bruce, Bishop of Dunkeld, appointed Gilbert Steward and John Steward, his son, as conjoint commissary-clerks of Dunkeld. Although John Steward was only an infant, he was ordered to continue to hold office, even though his father should die. However, upon the death of the father in August 1687 the new bishop, John Hamilton, disallowed the

---

[1] *Lauderdale Papers*, II, 239-40.

claim and his action was upheld by the Lords.[1] Such appointments, however, were not common. More serious was the accusation by Leighton in 1673 concerning a vacant "Comissariate, though one of ye meanest, [yet] more was offered mee by some of the competitors then I think one much better were worth, if sett to sale in ye market-place, & I think it a shamefull abuse that Churchmen should so comonly doe soe by these places, disposing them to any man more bids, and I heartily wish this were discharg'd".[2]

In some see cities, the bishops had the right to appoint the provost, baillies, and other officers of the city. On 20 May 1661 Parliament ratified the ancient right of the "Bishop of Aberdein for the tyme and his successors Bischops thairof full power and libertie of choiseing appointing and ordaineing yeerly the said Provest Baillies Seriands and other necessar officars, and of imputing and removeing the said persons how oft so ever they should find expedient".[3] The Bishop of Aberdeen exercised this right during this period. On 24 October 1668 the council minutes report that

. . . Maister Androw Moore and William Forbes tuo of the tounes baillies demitted ther offices off baillierie . . . and sent Androw Cassie and William Angus deacon conveiner to my lord bischop to signifie the samen to his Lo. to the effect his Lo. might elect uthers in ther places . . . who accordinglie did the same.[4]

Apart from these elections, however, it is interesting to note that the burgesses had almost complete freedom from any episcopal control of their activities, and the minutes of the council show that the bishop interfered only on rare occasions.[5] The Archbishop of Glasgow also had the right to name the provost, baillies, and other officers of the city. It was typical of Robert Leighton, as Archbishop of Glasgow, to seek to share this authority. The following minute of the Town Council is dated 1 October 1672:

The quhilk day, being the ordinarie day for the electioune of the magistratis of this burgh of Glasgow for a year to come, there was

[1] *Dunkeld*, I, 328–9.
[2] *Lauderdale Papers*, II, 239.
[3] *Records of Old Aberdeen*, I, 21–2.
[4] Ibid., p. 117.
[5] Ibid., preface. See also pp. 99–151.

sent doune, be the archbishop of Glasgow his servant, ane paper
subscribit by the said archbishop of this dait, bearing him to desyre,
for this tyme . . . to know quhom the toune counsell of Glasgow
. . . doe desyre to be thair magistratis for the enshewing year, and
that they meit for this end, trusting they will be carefull to manage
this affair without tumult. And first, he desyred to know, as being
himselfe impartiall in that, whom they wold have their proveist, and
the persone whom they should recommend, (unles his grace upon
verie weightie reasons to the contrair) sall lykly be nominat be the
said archbischop.[1]

William Andersoune was recommended for re-election as
Provost and the Archbishop appointed him.

This procedure was certainly a very different one from that
which Alexander Burnet had followed as Archbishop of Glasgow
in 1664. In August of that year it was reported that "these magistrates, viz. provest and bailleis, wer chosin by the Archebischop of
Glasgow, and by his awin autoritie, without the old forme of
electioune".[2]

Apart from their more formal civil and legal duties, the bishops
were important public figures of considerable influence and position. When the old town of Aberdeen was in danger of having its
liberties curtailed at Edinburgh in 1668, the Town Council
elected "William Forbes Thomas Angus and William Lind who
were ordaint to goe to the bishop and members of the colledge and
advyse wt them qt sould be done thereanent and qt course were
best to be taken".[3] One of the more interesting rights of the
Bishop of Aberdeen, which was confirmed by Act of Parliament in
1661, was the

priveledge libertie and power of buying all sorts of victuall wynes or
other merchandice brought within the Port of Aberdein . . . for
their oune comodious vtilitie both for the honest sustenations of
themselffs and families and for selling agane.[4]

---

[1] A slightly different procedure was followed the next year. At that time, the
"archbishop of Glasgow . . . grantit licence to the said magistrates and
counsell to sett doune a lyt of three persons out of quhilk lyt the said bishop
might choyse one persone to be proveist of this burgh the said year enshewing".
Glasgow Council Record. Quoted in Butler, *Life and Letters of Robert Leighton*, p. 495.
[2] Nicoll, p. 419.   [3] *Records of Old Aberdeen*, I, 22.   [4] Ibid.

Sometimes the influence of Scottish bishops upon their friends in England was used on behalf of their cities. On 9 August 1667 Archbishop Alexander Burnet wrote to Archbishop Sheldon that "I must beg your Gr/ advice and assistance for obtaining that mortified money is due by the E. of Argile to our citty of Glasgow".[1] In 1680 the Privy Council ordered "that the gazettes and news-letters read in coffee-houses, be first presented to the Bishop of Edinburgh, or any other privy councillor, that they may consider them, and thereby false and seditious news and slanders be prevented".[2] At times the bishops took a very active part in the tumultuous proceedings of the time. On 8 December 1666 Archbishop Burnet wrote to the Archbishop of Canterbury that he was in Glasgow during the rebellion of November last. "Before I was perfectly recovered of my fever I was constrained to make my house a garrison, and to appoint guards of horse and foot to secure our towne from a sudden surprisall, wch through God's blessing succeeded well with us."[3] One of the more interesting of such endeavours was that of Archbishop Sharp during the war with Holland in 1665–7. A number of Scottish coastal cities had fitted out *cappers* or sailing vessels of one hundred to two hundred tons for privateering upon the Dutch merchantmen. A contemporary journal reported that

Not a sea cost town but rickt a capper out . . . and many rich commodities and a number of excellent vessells taken from the Dutch. . . . The Archbishop of St Andrewes had a stout caper under Captain Fleming at sea, which did much mischeefe. A smart waggish poet gave his Grace this pretty sarcasm:

At first apostles fishers were of men:
Oures catch by caping, thers by preaching then.
Those in old times did by a happye hand
The gospell preach almost in everye land!
But the wid Ocean shall hereafter be
The great Archbishop of Saint Andrews see:
His Grace is James by the mercy off God
Whilst he uppon the land makes his abode,

---

[1] *Lauderdale Papers*, II, Appendix, xlviii.   [2] *Domestic Annals*, II, 361.
[3] *Lauderdale Papers*, II, Appendix, xli.

But when a caping on the sea he posts,
He is the high priest of the Lord of Hosts

.   .   .   .

[For] he'll advise, Boates onely take, youl hear
Our Peter will cut off but Malchus eare:
And then the King will say, to end this meeter,
If't please your Grace put up your spurtle, Peter! [1]

It seems clear, therefore, that the bishops were not simply figureheads, but that they occupied an important and influential place within the civil government of Scotland at this time. They held and controlled important positions within the legislative, executive and judicial branches of the Government, and were in every sense the lords spiritual of the kingdom.

No account of the position of the bishops in Scotland would be complete without a thorough recognition of the extent of royal absolutism under which a bishop lived. The Parliament in 1661 had required an oath of allegiance which acknowledged the King to be "supreme governor of this kingdom, over all persons, and in all causes".[2] This, however, was considerably enlarged by the famous Assertory Act of 1669 which declared that

his Majestie hath the Supream Authority and Supremacie over all persons and in all causes ecclesiasticall within this kingdom; And that by vertew therof the ordering and disposall of the externall government and policie of the Church doth propperlie belong to his Majestie and his successours. . . . And that his Majestie . . . may setle, enact, and emit such constitutions, acts and orders, concerning the administration of the externall government of the Church, and the persons imployed in the same, and concerning all ecclesiasticall meitings and maters to be proposed and determined therein, as they in their royall wisdome shall think fit.[3]

It is not surprising that Lauderdale should write to Charles on 16 November 1669 that this Act

makes you Soveraigne in the Church, you may now dispose of Bishops & Ministers, and remove & transplant them as you please (which I doubt yow can not doe in England). In a word this Church, nor no

---

[1] *Chronicles of the Frasers*, p. 486.   [2] Wodrow, *History*, I, 92.
[3] *Source Book of Scottish History*, III, 160.

meeting nor Ecclesiastick Person in it, can ever trouble you more unles yow please. . . .[1]

It was believed by some churchmen that not only did this Act establish absolute royal control over the ecclesiastical government of the Church, but that it also gave the Crown the right to change the nature of that government at will.

On 20 December 1688 John Paterson, Archbishop of Glasgow, tried to explain in a letter to Sancroft the reason why some of the bishops of Scotland did not offer more resistance to the Roman policy of James VII. He reminded Sancroft of the "unequall circumstances and ground of law upon which Episcopacie stands in England from these upon which it is founded here" and then referred to the Assertory Act.

> The King's supremacie, by the first Act of Parliament, 1669, is so asserted and establisht, that by the words of that law, it is in the King's power not onlie to dispose of the persons and places of all Bishops at his pleasure, by removing them from their offices and benefices, (and accordinglie, the late King and this have been in constant possession of so doing,) but even to change Episcopacie it self into anie other form of government. Now this cannot be legallie done in England, your Lordships offices and benefices being secured by the right of a freehold; and when your rights are invaded, the nobilitie and gentrie of England are readie and zealous to owne and support you in them; but here, if the Court chance to frowne on us, it is farr otherwise, to say no worse, so that our Bishops here ly open to farr greater tentations to yeeld to the importunities of Court than yours doe.[2]

The circumstances under which the Assertory Act was passed make it clear that its primary purpose was to establish royal absolutism over the establishment and especially over the bishops. Lauderdale had begun to support a more conciliatory policy toward nonconformity—a change which was much opposed by the bishops, especially Archbishop Burnet of Glasgow. In September 1669 the Synod of Glasgow protested the royal indulgence of the previous June. Burnet presided over that synod. The Privy Council

---

[1] *Lauderdale Papers*, II, 164.   [2] Clarke, *Collection of Letters*, 93–4.

C

declared that the protest was of a dangerous and illegal character, ordered it to be suppressed, and banished Archbishop Burnet to his diocese. When Parliament opened in the following month, its first Act was the Assertory Act. Two months later, on 2 December 1669, Charles ordered Burnet to be deprived of his jurisdiction.

> Having considdered the paper past in name of the Archbishop & Synode of Glasgow, & Our Privy Council's opinion concerning the same (wch opinion wee do heartily approve). . . . Wee do fine that the Archb's carryage hath contributed to the formenting [of the disorders in that Diocese], & do therefore on all these grounds esteem him unfit to govern that sea any longer. Therefore wee do require you to call him before you, & in presence of the Archb. of St Andrew's & such other of the Bishops as you think fit, to express our Ressentments. . . . And though . . . [this] were sufficient to inferr a guilt of a higher nature than wee are willing to charge him with; yet wee shall be content to accept of a Dimission & Resignation of his Bishoprick in our hands, & that no further prosecution be of the said matters (you alwise discharging him of his attendance at Our Privy Council).[1]

Burnet's suspension continued for four years, until in September 1674 he was restored to his jurisdiction by royal letter.

On several other occasions the royal authority frowned upon the episcopate in a similar manner. In 1674 Bishop Ramsey of Dunblane (who had been recommended to that see by Robert Leighton) incurred the royal displeasure, as well as that of his Primate, for supporting a movement to call a National Synod. On 16 July 1674 Charles declared

> that it is our royal pleasure, that forthwith there be a translation of the bishop of Dunblane, to that of the Isles . . . and we do positively require you to cause the bishop of Dunblane, within two weeks to remove from residence in any place of the diocese of Glasgow, and forbear meddling with matters relative to the church, save in his diocese of the Isles.[2]

Instead of repairing to the Isles, the Bishop of Dunblane journeyed to London to plead his cause. After numerous negotiations and a submission by Ramsey, he was restored to his see in April 1676.

---

[1] *Lauderdale Papers*, II, 167.   [2] Wodrow, *History*, II, 304.

James VII also made use of his ecclesiastical authority. In 1686 Bishop Bruce of Dunkeld was deprived for his opposition to the Roman policy of the Crown. The see was offered to James Drummond, Bishop of Brechin, but he refused, saying he knew of no vacancy there. John Hamilton, a minister of Edinburgh, had no such scruples and was consecrated at St Andrews on 4 November. Interestingly enough, a royal letter of 15 August 1687 gave a dispensation to Bruce, late Bishop of Dunkeld, to exercise his ministry, and on 4 May 1688 he was translated to the see of Orkney.

Bishop Bruce was not the only one in the reign of James VII to know royal disfavour. On 13 January 1687 Alexander Cairncross, Archbishop of Glasgow, was deprived for failing to censure Dr James Canaries, who had preached a sermon against popery.

The more important of the lesser clergy were also made aware of the extent of royal control. The letter which exiled Ramsey to the Isles also ordered disciplinary transfer for four leading ministers who had supported the bishop—Burner, Robertson, and Cant from Edinburgh, and Hamilton from Leith.

On only one occasion did the bishops manage to oppose government policy with any success. The Parliament of 1686 rejected the Toleration Act of James VII. Although the Primate, Alexander Burnet, and Alexander Rose, Bishop of Edinburgh, had previously agreed while in London to toleration of the Papists, yet episcopal opposition to the Toleration Act was not lacking. Among the opposing bishops was Atkins, Bishop of Galloway, who "though he was so enfeebled by age and sickness that he could not walk, was carried daily to the Parliament House".[1] Wodrow wrote:

> . . . I hear Bishop Atkin of Galloway, an old man, made a noble stand, and died shortly after; otherwise probably he had been turned out. And Bishop Bruce of Dunkeld, who had a remarkable sermon at that time, much commended, opposed the [repeal of the] penal statues, and was put from his office. I find Bishop Ramsay of Ross used great freedom with the Commissioner, and came to no small trouble therefore.[2]

[1] "A Seventeenth Century Bishop: James Atkine, Bishop of Galloway", *Scottish Historical Review*, January 1915, p. 135.
[2] Wodrow, *History*, IV, 365.

The crucial vote took place in the Committee of the Articles when four of the six bishops present voted against it, the Bishop of Dunkeld having been previously expelled for his opposition.

Opposition to this extent had not occurred since the Restoration, and the ordinary policy of both Parliament and the bishops was active support of or at least compliance with, the royal programme.

The treatment of nonconformity was one of the most important problems which both the Government and the bishops had to face. The various policies of the period, whether of repression or conciliation, were largely determined by the Government. Nonconformity had obvious political overtones, and the armed character of the later conventicles, as well as the two insurrections, would hardly allay the suspicions of the Government that nonconformity was really rebellious in character. The claim of *The Prelatical Churchman* (1690) that "Let 'em talk what they will, he who hates a bishop can never love a King", and of the *Memorial for the Prince of Orange* (1689) that not one Covenanter "suffered either ecclesiastick or civil censure only upon that account but for high treason against the State", is well paralleled in charges before the Privy Council such as "haunting field conventicles and evill affected to his majesties government and peace of the countrie".[1]

Royal absolutism over the Church is well illustrated by the inability of the bishops to influence the Government's attitude toward nonconformity. By and large the bishops were in favour of the policy of repression, and were quite unable to prevent the conciliation policy of 1667–74. The Archbishop of St Andrews, James Sharp, wrote to Archbishop Sheldon in 1666 that

> It is to me matter of admiration how in a tym so uncertain and palpably declyning to disobedience and contempt of the lawes, yt the King's ministers, especially persons of noble blood and abilities, doe not more vigorously and avowedly bestirr themselves for the opposing and suppressing that spirit which hath been so fatal to monarchy and nobility in these late times, and yet is not without hope and attempting to return to its beloved anarchy and chism.[2]

[1] Quoted in Henderson, *Religious Life in Seventeenth-Century Scotland*, pp. 182–3.
[2] *Lauderdale Papers*, II, Appendix, xxxix.

It is well known that Archbishop Burnet of Glasgow was deprived for his opposition to the First Indulgence. A further hint as to Burnet's attitude is found in the records of the Magistrates of Glasgow. In 1666 the Archbishop wrote to them complaining of the "several persons, men and women, who ordinarily dishaunts public ordinances, and flatters themselves with hope of impunity" and threatened to use the militia "both to observe who withdraws from ordinances and to exact the penalties imposed by law" if the magistrates did not enforce the law. Whereupon the magistrates resolved to take steps to collect the fines for non-attendance at church, this being much better "than that any solgers should have the collecting thereof".[1]

Toleration was not favoured by any of the religious parties in Scotland. In 1660, when some Scottish clergy still hoped for a purely presbyterian settlement, Robert Douglass wrote to James Sharp warning him against a policy of toleration. "He [Charles] needs not declare any liberty to tender consciences here, because the generality of the people and whole ministry have embraced the established religion by law. . . . It is known, that in all the times of the prevailing of the late party in England, none here petitioned for toleration, except some inconsiderable naughty men."[2] It is not surprising, therefore, that in the Restoration period the bishops, for the most part, should look upon the Covenanters as politically dangerous and ecclesiastically subversive, and that they should support the Government in its repressive measures.

A few members of the episcopal bench had reservations about the policy of repression. On 11 July 1676 the Presbytery of Dundee recorded that "The brethren in the Diocie of Dunkell refused to make publick intimation of the Act of the Synod annent schismaticks in regard the Bishop of Dunkell, their Ordinar, enjoyned the contrarie."[3] The Bishop of Dunkeld was Henry Guthrie, one of the more outstanding Restoration bishops, and the Act of the Synod "annent schismaticks" was an Act passed by Archbishop

---

[1] *Domestic Annals*, II, 305.   [2] Wodrow, *History*, I, 22.
[3] *Dunkeld*, I, 189.

Sharp and the Synod of St Andrews enjoining the most severe ecclesiastical penalties against nonconformity. George Wishart, the Bishop of Edinburgh, was imprisoned in the Thieves' Hole in the Tolbooth of Edinburgh in 1644, and "is said to have carried the marks of the rats' teeth to his grave". In 1665, when the prisoners from the First Insurrection were imprisoned in the Tolbooth, Wishart, perhaps remembering his own imprisonment there, sent food daily to the prisoners.[1]

The most important attempt to support another policy by any Restoration bishop was the Accommodation Scheme of Archbishop Leighton. Leighton was always critical of the policy of persecution. Even after the failure of the scheme and his retirement to England, he wrote:

> What pitifull poor things are wee if in our higher stations in ye world and particularly in ye church, wee project no higher end, then to drive poor people about us into a forc't complaince . . . ye french persecution is another mad frisk on thes stage.[2]

His reasons for opposing repression are important. They were based not so much upon an indifference to the issues involved as upon a belief that the existence of conflict and strife was destroying true religion on all sides. His sermon to Parliament on 14 November 1669 makes this quite clear:

> If it be the mind of God that that Order, which from the primitive times has been in constant succession in this and other Churches, do yet continue, what is that to thee or to me? If I had one of the loudest, as I have one of the lowest voices, yea, were it as loud as a trumpet, I would employ it to sound a retreat to all our unnatural and irreligious debates about religion and to persuade men to follow the meek and lowly Jesus. There is great abatement of the inwards of religion, when the debates about it pass to a scurf outside, and nothing is to be found within but a consuming fever of contention, which tendeth to utter ruin. If we have not charity towards our brethren, yet let us have some compassion towards our mother.[3]

---

[1] "Montrose's Chaplain", *Records of the Scottish Church History Society*, v, 42–3.
[2] *Miscellany of the Scottish History Society*, ii, 362.
[3] Butler, *Life*, pp. 420–21.

Leighton's Scheme was a proposal to reduce the character of the Settlement to a moderate episcopacy and to convince the Covenanters that such a moderate episcopacy was not contrary to their conscience or principles. In *A Defence of Moderate Episcopacy* he argued that the National Covenant, while it rejected prelacy on the English model, did not repudiate moderate or parochial episcopacy. He pointed out that English Presbyterians at the Restoration, including Richard Baxter, were willing to accept such episcopacy.

The proposed terms of the Accommodation on 9 August 1669 are described by Burnet:

He [Leighton] proposed that the church should be governed by the bishops and their clergy mixing together in the church judicatories, in which the bishop should act only as president, and be determined by the majority of his presbyters, the presbyterians should be allowed, when they sat down first in these judicatories, to declare that their sitting under a bishop was submitted to by them only for peace sake, with a reservation of their opinion with relation to any such presidency: and that no negative vote should be claimed by the bishop: that bishops should go to the churches where such as were to be ordained were to serve, and hear and discuss any exceptions that were made to them, and ordain them with the concurrence of the presbytery: and such as were to be ordained should have leave to declare their opinion, if they thought the bishop was only the head of the presbyters. And he also proposed that there should be provincial synods, to sit in course every third year, or oftener if the king should summon them; in which complaints of the bishops should be received, and they should be censured accordingly.[1]

At a meeting six months later, Leighton made a few further concessions, but the Accommodation was satisfactory to neither side. Leighton's fellow-bishops were hardly pleased with a scheme which even Gilbert Burnet admitted "left little more than the name of a bishop",[2] while the Covenanters (although some among them were indulged clergy) replied that "We are not free in

[1] Burnet, *History*, II, 497–8. See also Butler, *Life*, pp. 444–52.
[2] Burnet, *History*, II, 498.

conscience to close with the Propositions made by the Bishop of Dunblane as satisfactory".[1]

A vivid description of one of the meetings was given by the Reverend John Law in a letter to Lady Cardrosse. After a long and full evening in which there was much argument on both sides,

> Mr. George Hutcheson gav a very free and full discourse, and told the Bishop that he now saw where to the accommodation tended, namely to bring them on to him and to cause them have better thoughts of episcopacie, and at lenth to burie presbiterian government with their oun consent. Mr. Mathew Ramsey also spake most freely, but Mr. Alexr Jamisone did so oppose the bishope that he ran out of the roome and held up his hands, crying "I see there will be no accommodation."[2]

The success of the Scheme was improbable from the start amid those times of suspicion and tumult, yet it is worthwhile noting that the one important attempt at real comprehension—an attempt which involved a very drastic reduction of the authority of the bishop—was proposed by the most outstanding of the Restoration bishops, Robert Leighton.

The changed attitude of the nobility towards episcopacy has already been noted.[3] The Presbyterian party in Scotland, as in England, discovered to their great surprise that the upper classes were no longer invariably anti-episcopal. In 1662, when Archbishop Sharp made his first journey from Edinburgh to St Andrews, he was accompanied by many of the nobility and gentry. "The anxiety of the upper classes to do honour to the new system is shewn in the cortege which accompanied the prelate next day to St Andrews. He had an earl on each hand, and various other nobles and lairds, and at one time between seven and eight hundred mounted gentlemen, in his train."[4]

---

[1] Butler, *Life*, p. 445.
[2] *Lauderdale Papers*, III, 234.
[3] See above, p. 2. For Wodrow's suggestions as to the reason for this change in the attitude of the nobility, see *History*, I, 89. See also the *Cambridge Modern History*, v, ch. 10 (2).
[4] *Domestic Annals*, II, 291.

Such enthusiasm did not continue. Opposition by the nobility to royal policy, especially as that policy was represented in the rule of Lauderdale, was growing throughout the period. Since bishops were inextricably bound up with the policy of the Crown, many of the nobility came to have considerable reservations about their earlier enthusiasm. Yet it was a tendency only. There was never any likelihood that the nobility would resort again to revolutionary activity to remove the bishops. And the events of the Revolution likewise demonstrated the uncertainty of the nobility on the wisdom of rejecting episcopacy. The Claim of Right which rejected "prelacy" was passed only after the important Jacobite minority had withdrawn.

Clearly the bishops of Scotland were important figures in the civil structure of the kingdom. Royal policy did dominate the episcopate on all major issues and no bishop was a great officer of state. Yet in the ordinary civil structure of society, the authority and influence of the bishops were considerable. Their work in Parliament and on the committees of Parliament, their control of the Commissary Courts, and their influence as great citizens of the kingdom make clear the reality of episcopal restoration. Once again, bishops exercised something like their powers of old and took no small part within the civil life of the realm as the "first and spiritual estate".

3

BISHOPS AND THE KIRK

THE medieval diocesan structure of Scotland survived with little change through the sixteenth and seventeenth centuries. The archiepiscopal see of St Andrews was divided by Charles I in 1633, and the diocese of Edinburgh was created. With this exception the main geographic units continued, whether they were called synod, province or diocese.

Scotland was divided into two provinces, St Andrews and Glasgow, and into fourteen dioceses. The Province of St Andrews included the dioceses of Aberdeen, Brechin, Caithness, Dunblane, Dunkeld, Edinburgh, Moray, Orkney, Ross, and St Andrews, while the Province of Glasgow included Argyll, Galloway, Glasgow, and the Isles. The Bishops of Edinburgh and Galloway took precedence after the Archbishops.

Bishops were appointed by the Crown, the method of appointment being regulated, with one minor exception, by the Act of Parliament of 1617 "Anent the Electioune of Archbischopes and Bischopes". On the death of a bishop, a *congé d'élire* was sent to the Dean and Chapter authorizing them to hold a new election. At the same time a letter was sent nominating and recommending the person to be elected. At the meeting of the Chapter the candidate nominated was elected and the election certified. Royal assent to the choice was given under the Great Seal, and the person elected was thereby entitled to the temporalities of the see for life. A mandate was issued to a sufficient number of bishops to perform his consecration according to "the rites and ordoure accustumed".

At the Restoration, Chapters did not exist and the bishops were appointed directly by the Crown. After the re-establishment of Chapters, the procedure outlined above was followed.[1]

[1] *Dunkeld*, I, 49.

During the Restoration period, the Primate of Scotland, the Archbishop of St Andrews, exercised a surprising amount of influence on the choice of the bishops. On 9 October 1662 a letter to Sharp from Lauderdale expressed the hope that the Archbishop would "be pleased to receave thretteen of the fourteen presentations wch you sent me. Yor brother will tell you why the other was stopt."[1] Equally surprising is the discovery that Lauderdale's recommendations were often ignored. On 4 February 1663 Lauderdale wrote to Sharp that

> I need not put you in minde how advantageous I conceave it wodl be for the good of the Church if the Bp of Edr were provided with Orkney, if it can be with his good liking. You are the onely person can order that matter, and till I heare from you I shall say no more.[2]

Significantly, George Wishart, the Bishop of Edinburgh, was not translated to Orkney. Even when Lauderdale gained more influence, he still wrote to Sharp (on 30 January 1666) that "No Bp shall be offered by me to any vacancie but whom you Gr. shall first recomend".[3] In 1671 Lauderdale's advice was again ignored. On 29 August he wrote to Sharp that "now Edr is voyd . . . but in generall I thinke it not fitt at all that any presbitir should be at first dash prefer'd to Edr. It wold looke like ane injurie to the rest of the Bishops."[4] In spite of this advice, Alexander Young, Archdeacon of St Andrews, was consecrated Bishop of Edinburgh by the end of the year.

There was one man, however, whose translation Archbishop Sharp was unable to prevent. An order was issued in 1671 for the translation of Robert Leighton to the archiepiscopal see of Glasgow, and Sharp could only reply that I "shall obey the command for translation, though I differ from the new Archbishop as to his proposals for accommodation".[5] This was an unusual case, for as late as 1676 Lauderdale assured Sharp that "I am authorized by his Majtie to tell you . . . that he will not signe (as I am

---

[1] *Miscellany of the Scottish History Society*, I, 252.
[2] Ibid., p. 255.
[3] Ibid., p. 260.
[4] Ibid., p. 267.
[5] Ibid.

sure I shall not offer) any presentation in favours of any person but such as shall have the approbation of the two Arch Bishops within their respective Provinces. . . ."

In the latter years of the period there were signs of more lay influence. Thus on 25 January 1678 Sharp received a notice that the King had heard of the death of the Bishop of Ross, and had decided to translate the Bishop of Edinburgh to Ross and the Bishop of Galloway to Edinburgh.[1] The new Bishop of Edinburgh was John Paterson, who, through the powerful patronage of Lauderdale, was advanced from the deanery of Edinburgh to the bishopric of Galloway in 1674; from there to Edinburgh in 1679; and then to the archbishopric of Glasgow in 1687.[2] Nevertheless, in view of the very great influence which Sharp exercised over the nomination of bishops, he must share part of the blame for the generally mediocre calibre of the Scottish bench.

Episcopal lands were confiscated in 1587,[3] but James VI made a real attempt to restore them in the first decades of the seventeenth century.[4] The bishops received income from the rents of those lands which were restored and from certain assigned teinds or tithes. During the Interregnum episcopal revenues were devoted to various purposes. The City of Edinburgh received the incomes of the bishoprics of Orkney and Edinburgh. On 6 September 1661 the Privy Council ordered that "the rentis belonging to severall Bischoprikes and Deanreis be restored and maid vesfull to the Churche according to justice and the standing law".[5] In the diocese of Galloway the bishop received rents and teinds from the priory of Whithorn and the abbacies of Tongland and Glen-

---

[1] *Miscellany of the Scottish History Society*, I, pp. 272, 276.

[2] Apparently lay influence continued to dominate the presentations, since in 1682 Alexander Burnet, now Archbishop of St Andrews, wrote to Sheldon in England: "I must entreat your Grace to advise his Majestie not to dispose of Bishopricks till we be heard, for those that are obtruded on us by . . . great men . . . neither dare nor will be just and faithfull to the Church, as we have found in many instances. . . ." Clarke, *Collection of Letters*, 52.

[3] By the Act of Annexation. See *Source Book of Scottish History*, III, 44.

[4] See the Act for the Restitution of the Estate of Bishops, *Source Book of Scottish History*, III, 57.

[5] Nicoll, p. 341.

luce, as well as from some lands belonging to the bishopric itself.[1]

The income of the bishops varied widely. At the top of the scale were five sees with fairly substantial incomes: St Andrews with 1150*l. sterling*, Glasgow with 810*l.*, Edinburgh with 720*l.*, Galloway with 520*l.*, Orkney with 580*l.*, and Ross with 495*l.* The remaining dioceses had much smaller incomes—Aberdeen with 300*l.*, the Isles with 280*l.*, Brechin with 200*l.*, Moray and Caithness with 190*l.* each, Dunkeld with 150*l.*, Argyll with 140*l.*, and Dunblane with 105*l.*[2] Even Wodrow is led to comment that "I suppose I will not be much out when I say the bishopric of Winchester is better than all our Scots bishoprics put together".[3]

An Englishman who visited Scotland during the period suggested that the upper-income bishops had enough to live on.

> Their Revenues are not great, yet valuable considering the countrey. 1000*l. sterling* per Year for an Archbishop, and 5 or 600 for a Bishop, is thought a Competency where Provision is very cheap, and a good Table kept with little charges.[4]

The lower-income bishops found it difficult to manage, and, in order to supplement their incomes, sometimes were also ministers of parishes, occasionally of more than one. David Fletcher, Bishop of Argyll, continued as the minister of Melrose until his death.[5] The Bishop of Brechin was also the minister of the Kirk of Brechin, First Charge. George Haliburton, Bishop of Brechin, was presented by Charles II as Minister of Coupar Angus in 1680 "in respect the Bishopric is small and inconsiderable, so that it is very incompetent for maintaining of a Bishop in the dignity due to his sacred character".[6] Andrew Wood, Bishop of the Isles, received a royal dispensation to continue "his former liveing at Dunbar".[7] The Bishops of Dunkeld were also usually the ministers of Meigle,[8] and the Bishops of Moray were ministers of Elgin.[9]

---

[1] Register of Deeds, 21 March 1684, quoted in "A Seventeenth-Century Bishop", *Scottish Historical Review*, January 1915.
[2] *Dunkeld*, I, 50–51.   [3] Wodrow, *History*, I, 235.
[4] Morer, *Short Account of Scotland*, p. 50.   [5] *Dunkeld*, I, 51.
[6] *Fasti*, v, 392.   [7] *Miscellany of the Scottish History Society*, I, 276.
[8] *Dunkeld*, I, 51.   [9] *Elgin*, II, 390.

Charles was aware of the poverty of these bishoprics, and was even willing to do something about it. A royal dispensation for additional livings was fairly easy to secure, but perhaps something more may be implied in a letter from Alexander Burnet of St Andrews to the Archbishop of Canterbury in 1682.

> And since his Highnesse [the Duke of York] returned to Court, he hath represented to his Majestie the deplorable condition of two of our Bishopricks, which were allmost wholly dilapidated, and now, by his Majestie's wonted grace and his Highnesse intercession, those two contemptible charges are in a faire way to be restored to their primitive condition, by which they will yeeld the incumbents a very comfortable maintaince. There is a third Bishopricke in a very low condition, which we hope his Highnesse will likewise endeavour to help.[1]

Some of the bishops who held an extra living fulfilled their duties as ministers of the kirk when they were present. The Bishop of Brechin usually lived at Meigle and regularly held services there. The Bishop of Moray lived at Elgin and acted as the parish minister. In 1666 the kirk-session of Elgin reported that Murdoch McKenzie, Bishop of Moray, "preaches regularly every Sunday forenoon".[2] He presided over the meetings of the kirk-session, and although not the official moderator of the presbytery of Elgin, he presided over the meetings of that body, too, when present.[3]

Some of the bishops had their permanent residence outside their diocese. Charles had written that "none of our archbishops or bishops may lawfully keep their ordinary residence without the bounds of their respective diocese, unless they have our royal dispensation, warrant, and licence for that effect . . .",[4] yet such licences were fairly common. Bishop Atkins, translated to Galloway in 1680 at the age of sixty-six, was given a special dispensation to live in Edinburgh

> because it was thought unreasonable to oblige a reverend prelate of his years to live among such a rebellious and turbulent people

[1] Clarke, *Collection of Letters*, p. 42.   [2] *Elgin*, II, 305.   [3] Ibid., p. 374.
[4] Stephen, *Life and Times of Sharp*, p. 568. See also *Dunkeld*, I, 52, n. 2.

as those of that diocese were: the effects of whose fiery zeal hath too frequently appeared in affronting, beating, robbing, wounding, and sometimes murdering the curates.

He made one visit to his diocese, though with "great pains in undertaking a very great journey for a man of his age and infirmities", and otherwise governed the diocese by "pastoral letters to the Synod, presbyteries and ministers".[1] Candidates for ordination made the trip to Edinburgh, and were ordained by him there.[2]

Sydserf, the aged Bishop of Orkney, lived at Edinburgh, and Andrew Honeyman, his successor, lived at St Andrews. Fletcher, Bishop of Argyll, resided at his parish of Melrose, and Wood, Bishop of the Isles, lived at his parish in Dunbar.[3]

The surprising thing about this list is its brevity. Records of other cases of non-residence may simply have disappeared, but at least most of the other bishops maintained a home in their diocese and were there for part of the year. It is clear that much of the year, however, was spent in Edinburgh. In 1664 Sharp wrote that he planned to spend the period from April to June in Fyfe (St Andrews). The remainder of the year would be spent at Edinburgh. This was probably his usual practice.[4] An examination of the letters of Archbishop Burnet of Glasgow from 1664 until 1667 shows that he was ordinarily in Glasgow about one month each year, usually in May.[5] During the rest of the year he could usually be found in Edinburgh. As members of the Privy Council, the two archbishops would be more frequently in Edinburgh than other members of the bench. However, even when Parliament was not in session, a number of the bishops remained there. In 1680 three encyclical letters were sent from Scotland to the bishops of England and from five to eight bishops were present to sign them.[6] In 1668 the Earl of Tweeddale casually referred to

---

[1] "A Seventeenth-Century Bishop", *Scottish Historical Review*, January 1915, p. 139.
[2] Keith, *Historical Catalogue of the Scottish Bishops*, p. 282.
[3] *Dunkeld*, I, 51. [4] *Lauderdale Papers*, I, 195.
[5] Ibid., II, Appendix A.
[6] Clarke, *Collection of Letters*, pp. 8, 13, 21.

the "10 or 12 of the B; who have bein in toune this two month",[1] even though Parliament was not in session. Yet the synod records which are available indicate that the bishop held an annual or semi-annual synod with remarkable regularity, and most of the bishops must have paid at least an annual visit to their dioceses.

Knowledge of the form and manner of consecration of the bishops of Scotland during the Restoration is singularly meagre. At the Restoration only one bishop of Scotland was still living: Thomas Sydserf, the Bishop of Galloway. Therefore the first Restoration bishops were called to England for their consecration.

When the four candidates arrived, it was discovered that two of them, Sharp and Leighton, had not received episcopal ordination to the diaconate or priesthood. Sharp claimed the precedent of Spottiswood, who in 1610 had only received presbyterian ordination, but was none the less consecrated *per saltum* by the English bishops. The precedent was disallowed and the English bishops maintained that in the time of King James

> . . . they [the Scots] had been under a real necessity [and] it was reasonable to allow of their orders, how defective soever; but that of late they had been in a state of schism, they had revolted from their bishops, and had thrown off that order: so that orders given in such wilful opposition to the whole constitution of the primitive church was a thing of another nature.[2]

Leighton's reply well reflects his attitude on such matters: "I will yield, although I am persuaded I was in orders before, and my ministrations were valid, and they do it *cumulative* and not *privative*: though I should be ordained every year I will submit." [3] There is no evidence that this practice was repeated in Scotland and that any consecrations there were preceded by episcopal ordination to the presbyterate.

After their ordination as deacons and priests, the four candidates were publicly consecrated in Westminster Abbey on the Third Sunday in Advent, 15 December 1661 by the Bishops of

---

[1] *Lauderdale Papers*, II, 114.
[2] Burnet, *History*, I, pp. 247–8. See also Wodrow, *History*, I, 239.
[3] Wodrow, *Analecta*, I, 133. Quoted in Butler, *Life*, p. 333.

London, Worcester, Carlisle, and Llandaff. Numerous descriptions of the consecration have survived. Nicoll's account is perhaps a good summary of the impression made upon a Scottish layman. "This consecration was actit with great solempnitie, in presence of many of the nobilitie and clergy of England, and many of the nobles of Scotland, being thair for the tyme attending his Majestie." [1]

It should be noted that in all probability the Edwardian ordinal was used at this London consecration. The revised ordinal was not adopted by Convocation until 20 December, and it did not receive Royal assent until May 1662. Thus, if the Scottish bishops took any English ordinal back with them to Scotland, it would probably have been the Edwardian ordinal.

It is much more difficult to determine what happened in Scotland during subsequent consecrations. The letters patent appointing bishops in 1662 stated that they were to be consecrated "according to the order of consecration heretofore used and received in the Church of Scotland". [2] This may refer to the Scottish Ordinal of 1620, but since there is a great deal of uncertainty about what was the "order of consecration heretofore used", the quotation tells us little about Restoration practice.

Most important is the statement made by Archbishop Paterson. On 6 July 1670 Charles II had referred in some instructions to "the form of ordination". Ten years later, Paterson in transcribing these instructions noted that "There is no form of ordination appointed to this day". [3] Nothing has been discovered which would contest the accuracy of this statement. Nor is it surprising that there should be no appointed form. The Church of Scotland had no official liturgy for any of its public services. [4] The absence of an official ordinal was quite consistent with the practice of the Restoration Church in the conduct of all its public services.

[1] Nicoll, p. 354. See also descriptions in Kirkton, *History*; Wodrow, *Analecta*, I, 133; and Butler, *Life*, pp. 333–4.

[2] H.M. Register House, Edinburgh, Paper Register of the Great Seal, v, 240. Quoted in Donaldson, "Scottish Ordinations in the Restoration Period", *Scottish Historical Review*, October 1954.

[3] Stephen, *Life of Sharp*, p. 432. Quoted from MS. in the Episcopal Chest. See also *Scottish Historical Review*, October 1954, p. 174.

[4] See below, p. 130.

D

Fortunately, accounts of some Scottish consecrations have survived. A contemporary description of the first consecration in Edinburgh on 7 May 1662 is given by Nicoll.

> The church of Halyrudhous being prepared and maid redy for thair consecratioun, numberis of pepill wer convenit, bot nane enterit the church bot such as haid pasportis. The 2 Archebischops went to the church in throw the Abay, clothed in thair quhyte surplechis under thair blak gownes except thair sleves, quhich were all of thame quhyte of diligat cambrige. . . . These that wer consecratouris wer the two Archebischops and Mr James Hammiltoun now Bischop of Galloway, quha ordored that bussines very handsumlie and decentlie. Befoir the consecratione, thair was a sermond maid by ane Mr James Gordoun. . . . The Archebischop of St. Androis sat thair coverced with his episcopall cap. . . . All that wes said by the Bischop at the consecratioun wes red af ane buik, and thair prayeris lykewyse wes red. The first prayer wes the Lordis prayer, and sum schoirt prayer of exhortatioun eftir that; nixt, wes the Beleiff red, and sum lytil exhortatioune eftir it; thridlie, the Ten Commandis red, and eftir it sum few wordis of exhortatioun;—much moir to this purpos, not necessar to be writtin.[1]

Two other early writers, both with strong covenanting sympathies, wrote about this consecration. William Row states that "the consecrators . . . made use of the Book of Ordination and Service Book and when they laid on their hands etc. . . . they said 'Receive ye the Holy Ghost'".[2] Wodrow also wrote that "the primate made use of the English forms, and read all from the book, the Lord's Prayer, Creed and Ten Commandments, and consecration and exhortation after it".[3] These statements show clearly some English influence. They also suggest that the Scottish ordinal of 1620 had much less influence, since the latter contained neither the Lord's Prayer, the Creed nor the Ten Commandments. However, they hardly imply an exact conformity to the English ordinal, and there is no evidence that the Holy Communion was celebrated, as required by both the English ordinal and the Scottish ordinal of 1620.

[1] Nicoll, pp. 365-6.
[2] *Life of Blair*, pp. 406-7. See also *Scottish Historical Review*, October 1954, p. 174.   [3] *History*, I, 255.

Evidence for later consecrations is very slight. There is a set of
scurrilous verses about a later consecration which alludes to the
Litany, the Creed, a sermon and a hymn, but little reliance can
be put on this. Clear evidence for the use of the English ordinal
exists only for the period after the Revolution, when a general
Anglicanizing of Scottish episcopacy was taking place. Thus in
1712, Bishop Ross held an ordination in Edinburgh which was
"according to the form of the Church of England".[1]

Additional evidence of Restoration practice is afforded by the
frequently discussed consecration of John Clement Gordon as
Bishop of Galloway on 19 September 1688. Gordon followed
James VII into exile and was later received into the Roman
Church. Shortly thereafter he petitioned for a declaration that his
consecration was "illegitimate and null" so that he could receive
"Holy Orders according to the Catholic rite". In his petition,
Gordon states that the form of ordination was "Take thou
authority to preach the Word of God and to minister His Holy
Sacraments".[2] Even if this is accurate, and it may well be,[3] the
English archbishops correctly noted that this is a form for ordina-
tion of a presbyter, not a bishop.[4]

Gordon's petition gives no information about his own consecration, but the Decision of Clement XI on Gordon's Petition,
issued on 17 April 1704, does contain such a description.

JOHN CLEMENT GORDON, a Scot, was ordained and consecrated
Bishop, or rather pseudo-Bishop, according to the Anglican rite,
September 19, 1688, in the Cathedral Church of Glasgow, in Scot-
land, by the pseudo-Archbishop and three pseudo-Bishops. The con-
secration took place as follows: *First,* Prayers were said from the
Anglican Liturgy. *Secondly,* a sermon was preached to the people on
the dignity and office of a Bishop. *Thirdly,* all the said pseudo-
Bishops láid their hands on the head and shoulders of the said John,

---

[1] *A true narrative of the case between the episcopal congregation in the Seagate of
Dundee . . . and Bishop Raitt,* Edinburgh, 1745, p. 30. See also *Scottish Historical Review,* October 1954, pp. 174-5.

[2] "Petition of John Clement Gordon, Bishop of Galloway, to the Holy
Office", printed in Lowndes, *Vindication of Anglican Orders,* II, cxvii ff.

[3] See below, p. 100.

[4] *Reply of the Archbishops,* Appendix, p. 62.

who was kneeling, with the words, " *Take the Holy Ghost, and remember that thou stir up the grace of God, which is in thee, by the imposition of hands; for God hath not given us the spirit of fear, but of power and love and of soberness.*" *Fourthly*, the service ended with a few prayers of thanksgiving.[1]

It is quite possible that this is an accurate description of Gordon's consecration. It would certainly be different from that prescribed by any English ordinal, and the archbishops in their "Answer" have little difficulty in pointing out the numerous incongruities. On the other hand, the account of Gordon's consecration records just the sort of thing which may well have gone on in Scotland. The "form" seems clearly derived from the Edwardian ordinal, and the whole service has obvious similarities with Nicoll's account of the Scottish consecrations of 1662.[2]

The authority of the Scottish bishops in the administration of the affairs of the Church was considerable during the Restoration period. In this area they were much less hampered by royal absolutism. The details of the exercise of this episcopal authority varied from place to place, but a general pattern of authority was established by Acts of Parliament and seems to have been more or less consistently followed throughout most of the country.

Much of the authority of the bishop was exercised in conjunction with the members of the synod. Almost universally, decisions

---

[1] Printed in Lowndes, *Vindication*, II, xcci.

[2] Incidentally, further knowledge of church life in Scotland in the Restoration may throw some light on the vexed question of Anglican orders. It is clear that Leo XIII regarded the Gordon case as quite crucial. Thus he stated: "Still more important it is to note that the judgment of the Pontiff [Clement XI's judgment on Gordon] applied universally to all Anglican ordinations because, although it refers to a particular case, it is not based upon any reason special to that case, but upon the defect of form, which defect equally affects all these ordinations: so much so that when similar cases subsequently came up for decision the same decree of Clement XI was quoted as the norma" ("Apostolicae Curae", pp. 8–9). Now, it is hoped that this thesis will make it increasingly clear that in no sense did Anglicanism exist in Scotland during the Restoration. Certainly Scottish consecrations, while showing signs of English influence, were quite different from those in the southern kingdom. Clement XI is not the only one to have confused the practice of the Church of England with the very different practice of the Church of Scotland. However, to use the case of a consecration in the Church of Scotland during the Restoration as evidence in judging the validity of English or Anglican orders is to use evidence of a singularly unsatisfactory kind.

of the diocesan synod were "enacted by the Bishope, with consent of the brethren of the Synod". Although this qualification on his authority was not required by Parliament, and whereas the bishop did possess a veto power over all actions of the synod, it is worth noting that episcopal authority within the Church was not quite as arbitrary as has sometimes been supposed.

In 1662 Parliament required all preachers, chaplains, public teachers, and tutors in families to obtain licences from the bishops of the dioceses.[1] This was duly noted in many of the synod meetings, and in the Synod of Aberdeen it was "enacted by the Bishope, with consent of the brethren of the Synod",[2] that each preacher who had his licence from the presbytery must get one *de novo* from "my Lord Bishope". In Banff, Mr Alexander Watt was told by the presbytery that he could not be admitted schoolmaster without taking the test (the Test Act of 1681), receiving their appointment, and getting approval from the bishop, for even "their act of councill nor his [Watt's] obligatione [to take the Test] can not louse him from obedience to the Lord Bishop of Aberdeen and canons of the Church qua schoolmaster of Bamfe".[3]

Although the bishop licensed the schoolmaster, the latter was usually first presented by the patron, and his trials or examination for admission were conducted by the presbytery. The whole procedure is well illustrated by the admission of Mr Francis Fordyce to the grammar school of Banff in 1673. The patrons presented Mr Fordyce to the Presbytery of Banff on 2 July 1673 and were told that they should present the candidate to the bishop, not the presbytery.

> They doubted not of ther right of presentatione, and wer glaid that the schooll did flourish . . . but that their advyce to them was that they wold mak first applicatione to the Lord Bishop, ther ordinarie, whose command they should verie readilie obtemper in that effair.[4]

On 9 September a dispute was reported in presbytery between the patrons and the Laird of Auchmedden, who wanted a Mr

[1] *Acts of Parliament*, VII, 376.
[2] *Records of Old Aberdeen*, II, 6.
[3] *Annals of Banff*, II, 55.
[4] Ibid., p. 41.

Alexander Mair chosen as schoolmaster. The whole dispute was referred to the bishop. On 12 November "Ane letter from the Lo/ Bishop was read wherein his Lo/ desyred that Mr Francis Fordyce, presented to the schooll off Banff, might be tryed . . .".[1] He was tried, and "gave satisfaction" on 10 December, was recommended to the Lord Bishop, and licensed later that month as the schoolmaster of Banff.

Not only did the bishop issue licences to preach, but he withdrew them if necessary. In the Presbytery of Inverness in 1673 Mr John Cuthbert violated an episcopal order and received the following letter from his bishop:

> . . . seeing ye haue been pleased to abuse that license granted to you by me, and with ane high hand verie contemptuouslie hes vilified and transgressed my order to you, I doe by these pnts suspend my licence of preaching granted to you, and I doe suspend you from preaching the gospell anywhere within this diocess of Morray untill the next Provinciall Synode to be holden at Elgine. . . . and I doe by these straitlie require you to compeir befor the Synode. . . . and I enjoyne the Modr of the exercise at Invernes to intimat this sentence to you presbyteriallie, lest you pretend ignorance of the same.[2]

In addition to licensed preachers and ministers, there was also a class of men known as readers or lectors who would read the Scriptures in the church on Sunday.[3] Usually these also were licensed by the bishop, but on unusual occasions they were simply licensed by the presbytery. In 1663 the Presbytery of Alford gave a licence to Mr David Milne of Glenbuchet "to read the Scripture in that Church on the Sabbath day till it shall please the Almightie to provide a minister for them", and went on to add that they gave him a licence "principally upon the account they hade no Ordinarie alive to whom they might recommend him for that licence".[4] The Bishop of Aberdeen had died the previous June.

A minister of a parish who was guilty of grave neglect of duty could expect severe disciplining from his bishop. Mr Michael

---

[1] *Banff*, II, p. 41.
[2] *Inverness and Dingwall*, p. 35.
[3] See below, pp. 128 ff.
[4] *Alford*, p. 10.

Fraser, Minister of Daviott in the Presbytery of Inverness, had a long history of absenteeism from his parish, of not celebrating the Lord's Supper, and of non-attendance at presbytery meetings. He was not well liked by the presbytery, and it was probably with some satisfaction that on 20 November 1678

the Moderator declared yt hee had received ane letter from my Lo. Bi. showeing yt Mr. Michael ffrasser, Minr. of Daviott, was suspended for a certaine tyme, and yt hee did wryte to Mr. Roderick McKenzie, minister at Moy, to repair to Daviott and there preach on ane Lords day, and to mak intimaon to the people off the sd paroch of the suspension of ther Minr. . . .[1]

The power to discipline ministers in this way rested in the hands of the bishop, and the presbytery was not allowed to exercise such drastic action by itself. For example, the Synod of Aberdeen declared that presbyteries "are not to censure any minister with suspensione or deprivatione without speciall warrand from the Bishope".[2] In 1684 the Presbytery of Dingwall reported that Mr John Gordon, Minister of Kilterne, was accused by Jean Bayne of being the father of her child. However, they decided that they could not censure Mr Gordon until he had been tried, "qch they judged could not be done by ym in the absence of yr Ordinary, or at least wtout a license from him; qrfore being for the present deprived of both, they suspend all future proceeding in yt affair till Providence sent yr Bp. amongst ym. . . ."[3]

Episcopal jurisdiction over the conduct of the clergy was not limited to the formal powers of suspension and deprivation, but was exercised in a multitude of ways. Thus on 3 January 1666 the Presbytery of Dundee reported that "the publication of the purpos of mariage [the banns] betwixt Mr James Campbell, minister at Aughterhous, and Dam Marjorje Ramsay . . . [was] stopped by ane order from the Right Reverend Father in God, the Bishop of Dunkeld, upon the account of ther scandal of fornication, till the scandal should be removd".[4] The conclusion of this case illustrates the way in which a bishop often worked with

---

[1] *Inverness and Dingwall*, p. 88.   [2] *Alford*, p. 3.
[3] *Inverness and Dingwall*, p. 351.   [4] *Dunkeld*, i, 189.

a presbytery in settling such matters. Licence was given by the bishop to the Presbytery of Dundee to see if Mr Campbell could be cleared of the scandal. They reported that they were able "to remove the scandal according to the order of the Church . . . [and] a liberty being granted by the Bishop of Dunkeld to the brethren of Dunde, they appoint the proclamations [the banns] to go on . . .".[1]

The very severe discipline of excommunication also required episcopal action. The Synod of Aberdeen declared that the presbyteries "shall not proceed to sentence any with excommunicatione, unless it be by order of the Bishope, after his lordship has visited and approven the process".[2] Nor was this authority exercised without some sense of the pastoral responsibilities involved. The Bishop of Galloway, in an undated letter written probably around 1685 to the Moderator of the Presbytery of Wigtoun about Elizabeth Steward, ordered "the relaxatione of hir from the sentence of excommunicatione pronounced Against hir by my predicesser [for] I judge that sentence too rigid". She was to be given some public censure, but of not too great severity. "Ye are to contract or prorog her tyme, according as ye find hir affected with sincere greife for hir sin, and hir heart to pant after reconciliatione with God and the Churches peace, that she may not be overwhelmed with greif." [3]

Where excommunication was obviously called for, it was sometimes imposed directly by the presbytery without any indication of episcopal approval. Thus the Presbytery of Elgin, on 31 May 1665 reported that "William Troupe in Elgin to be summarily excommunicat befor the nixt meeting. He was summoned for the sin of adultery but compeired not. Now he has added to his adulterie the crying sin of murther." [4]

---

[1] *Dunkeld*, I, 189.   [2] *Alford*, p. 3.
[3] *Miscellany of the Scottish History Society*, III, 94–5. A similar case occurred on 4 November 1674, when the Presbytery of Inverness reported "that, although there was an order for excommunicating Isobell Robertson in Kinmylies, that they were advised be the Bishope to delay the sentence, seeing they had some hopes of gaineing her from popery, and to be ane hearer". *Inverness and Dingwall*, p. 47.   [4] *Elgin*, II, 371.

Apart from episcopal supervision of the lower clergy and officers of the Church and the exercise of the highest censure of the Church —i.e. excommunication—we find the bishop engaged in a wide variety of activities concerned with the Church's administration and discipline. By Act of Parliament, kirk-sessions, presbyteries, and synods could meet only with episcopal approval, though such approval seems to have been universally given. The permanent moderators of presbytery were appointed by the bishop, and on the few occasions when the bishop was present at presbytery, he would preside himself. Synods were invariably presided over by the bishop, and they were not held if he could not be present.

Numerous problems were referred to him, especially matters for which there was no precedent or which were serious in themselves. In 1669 the Presbytery of Banff reported that "Eupham Ellies . . . [was] chairged with severall poynts off charmeing mad out against her befor the sessione [the kirk-session] of Banff. . . . The breethren, finding the mater weightie, resolued to carie in the paper presented to them from the sessione to the Lo/ Bishop and his Lo/ advyce may be had." [1] Two months later "the mynd of the Bishop and Synod" had been received, and presbytery acted on their directive. In 1675 it was reported of Mr Thomas Huistone to the Presbytery of Inverness that "he did never celebrat the sd sacrament in Kilchuming. [He] answered that he had not an kirk to celebrat it in, except he should celebrat it in the open fields, yt the Kirk was fallen. . . . The Bretheren referrs this case to the advise of ye Bishope and Synod, what shall such Bretheren do in reference to the celebratione of the Lords supper in such places as want an church to celebrat the same comelie and orderlie in." [2] On 21 April 1687 the Synod of Dunkeld recorded the "Erection of the Presbytery of Cowpar in Angus by the Bishop, with advice and consent of the Synod". [3] This was a new presbytery, usually known as Coupar Angus, made up of parishes from the Presbyteries of Perth, Dundee, and Dunkeld. [4] Difficult marriage cases were referred to the bishop. In June 1665 Mr John

[1] *Banff*, II, 40.
[2] *Inverness and Dingwall*, p. 55.
[3] *Dunkeld*, I, 319.
[4] Ibid., p. 401.

Mackenzie, Minister of Killearnan and Archdeacon of Ross, "advysed with the Presbyterie [of Dingwall] in reference to a woman in his Parish whose husband being caried to Barbados after the battell of Woster, and married ther for certainty, whether the said woman might haue the benefitt of marriage with another man; The Presbyterie . . . ordained the said Mr John to advyse with the Bishop heeranent." [1] Public projects were often supported under the direction of the bishop. On 16 November 1670 the Presbytery of Inverness "exhibited at the Presbytry directed from ye Bishop of Murray requiring a collection from ye respective Parishes within ye Presbytry for repairing of ye Bulwark of Dundye . . .".[2] The transfer of clergy to another parish required action of the bishop and synod. On 8 June 1670 Mr Thomas Huistone made a pitiful plea to the Presbytery of Inverness requesting transfer because of the violence of the community around him, "his house being laitly seized upon by Lochabber Robbers, himselfe threatened wt naked swords and drawne durks at his brest", but the brethren could give him little assistance.

> Ye Breyren, considering these sad reasons and condoling his condition, yet told him that they culd not give him ane Act of Transportation wtout ye Bishop and Synod's order, and therefor the Breyren requested him to haue patiently until the next Synod, casting himself upon the Lord for his shelter. . . .[3]

On 16 September 1674 the Minister of Banff reported to the Presbytery of Banff that "he had received from the Lo/ Bishop ane commissione and edict for designing of mosse [peat bog for fuel] to him out of the nixt adjacent [next parish]".[4]

One of the most important duties of the bishop was to act as a court of appeals for all major disciplinary cases. Bishop E. A. Knox suggests that the system of appeals used during the Interregnum may have broken down, inasmuch as there were cases of excommunication pronounced by "the minister with his council of twelve or fourteen elders". Such a sentence by a kirk-session,

---

[1] *Inverness and Dingwall*, p. 311.   [2] Ibid., p. 7.
[3] Ibid., p. 5.   [4] *Banff*, II, 42.

the lowest of four Church courts, was most unusual.[1] During the Restoration period, the authority of the episcopate made it impossible for the drastic punishment of excommunication to be imposed simply by one minister and his lay elders. In one area, the diocese of Aberdeen, a formal process of appeal existed. On 8 October 1668 the Synod of Aberdeen recorded that in the

> ordering the maters of appeall that shall happen in all tymes coming, within this diocie, (untill a more generall course be prescribed by the church thereanent) the Bishop doth give order and power to the respective Presbyteris to tak cognitione of, and cognosece, and judg such appealls as are made from the ministers, and particulare Sessiones within their bounds; and when any persone shall appeall from the Presbyterie to the Bishop, it is appoynted that the moderator of the Presbyterie shall acquaint the Bishop therwith, and that the Presbyterie desyst from any further processe against the said persone, untill they have received further order from the Bishop theranent.[2]

While such a formal system of appeal seems not to have existed in other dioceses, episcopal jurisdiction over the use of excommunication would mean that this gravest censure of the Church would not be imposed before the case was tried, or at least referred to the bishop.

It is clear that the bishop was far more than a mere figurehead within the Restoration Church. His responsibilities over the lower clergy went beyond the technical matters of licensing and transfer and included real oversight of the discipline and faithfulness of the clergy. His advice was sought on important or unusual matters, he presided over the most solemn assemblies held in the Restoration Church, and he dealt with all serious matters of discipline in which the laity were involved. Moreover, the bishops generally administered their duties in a responsible and serious manner. Matters referred from a presbytery were usually answered with reasonable promptitude, the bishop sometimes securing advice from the clergy, sometimes deciding by himself, sometimes consulting the synod, sometimes referring the matter back to the presbytery. There is also little evidence of conflict between the

[1] Knox, *Robert Leighton*, p. 142. [2] *Alford*, p. 130.

bishop and the lower courts. Although the Presbytery of Alford would have liked to continue action on the case of Mr Alexander Innes instead of permitting him to appeal to the bishop,[1] such evidences of friction are remarkably few. The general impression is one of considerable episcopal authority somewhat tempered by the "consent of the brethren of the Synod". It was an authority which was at least tolerable to those who conformed to the settlement and which was administered with a real degree of concern for the well-being of the Church.

Though formal visitation of the kirks was primarily the duty of the presbytery, this was usually carried out under licence of the bishop, who would exhort and require the presbyteries to fulfil their proper duties. On 17 April 1688 the Synod of Aberdeen recorded that the "Lord Bishop . . . seriously recommended to the severall Presbyteries to be deligent in going about the visitation of kirks within their respective bounds this summer, and that particular visitationes be kept at the kirks of such bretheren as are frequentlie absent from Presbyteries or Synods . . .".[2] However, the bishop himself was not always a complete stranger to the kirks of his diocese. Gilbert Burnet wrote that Robert Leighton "went round it [his diocese] constantly every year, preaching and catechising from parish to parish",[3] and this testimony is confirmed by Leighton's own letter to Lauderdale on 20 June 1674.

> I am minded God willing to go from hence within two or three days, to visit ye southern & remoter parts of ye diocese of Glasco, as I have formerly done in ye sumer season.[4]

On occasion a more formal visitation would be held by the bishop. On 18 April 1665 Archbishop Burnet wrote to the Archbishop of Canterbury that "I have beene of late at a visitan of the southern part of my diocese, and so could not attend the last counsell day . . .".[5] An example of such a tour is the visitation by Colin Falconar, Bishop of Moray, with the Presbytery of Inverness in 1682.

---

[1] *Alford*, pp. 114–15, 117, 132.   [2] Ibid., p. 389.
[3] *History*, I, 382.   [4] *Lauderdale Papers*, III, 56.
[5] Ibid., II, Appendix, xviii.

On 25 April 1662 the moderator reported to the presbytery that "the Bishop was resolved to enter his visitations in our Prebrie next month, and the first visitation to hold at Croy, May 15". The bishop did meet at Croy on 15 May with some presbyters from the Presbyteries of Elgin, Forres, and Abernethy, as well as with all the brethren of the Exercise (or Presbytery) of Inverness. The same group was at Daviot on 16 May, at Kirkhill on 17 May, and at Petty on 19 May.[1] On such visitations the bishop would invariably be accompanied by many of the presbytery, and the visitation would follow the same form as when held by the presbytery alone. A good example of such a visitation was that held by George Hallyburton, Bishop of Brechin, in Glen Ilo on 31 March 1680. After a sermon by Mr William Raitt of Kingoldrum, there was convened "in the kirk of Glenyla ane Reverend Father, George, be the mercie of God, Bishop of Brechin, the bretheren of the Presbetrie of Megill as assistants in the visitation, Mr David Nevay, minister, heritours and sessioners of Glenyla". After "prayer be the said Reverend Father" the session began. The heritors, who "with uplifted hands, did promise upon oath, as in the sight of God, to answer to the following", were individually examined about the life and faithful discharge of duties of the minister. The session book was examined and the minister himself questioned. It was discovered that the glebe and grass were according to law, but that the house was insufficient, that there was only five pounds *scots* in the poor-box, that there was no provision for a reader, and no roof on "the quire of the kirk". Whereupon the heritors were again called in by the bishop, who represented "unto them the insufficiencie of ther minister's house" and other defects. "They answered they would willingly goe about such a pious work" as reforming these abuses! "After prayer be the Bishop the meeting dissolved." On the following day, the bishop and brethren were at Kingoldrum, for the last visitation of the tour.[2]

The practice of confirmation is conspicuous by its absence. The

---

[1] *Inverness and Dingwall*, pp. 104–11.
[2] *Dunkeld*, II, 130–33.

nearest approach to it was a recommendation by Robert Leighton to the ministers of Dunblane

> that at the sett tymes of catechising and examineing their people that they would take particulare notice of young persones, and towards their first admissioun to the Holy Communion . . . and cause them each one particularly and expreslie to declaire their belieff of the Christiane faith into which in their infancie they were baptized and remynding them of that their baptismal vow. . . . And then, in their prayer with which they use to conclude these meetings, would recommend the said young persones now thus engagd to the effectual blessing of God, beseeching Him to owne them for His, and to bestowe on them the sanctifeing and strengthening grace of His Holie Spiritt, and His signature upon them sealling them to the day of redemption.[1]

There is no indication that this recommendation was very widely followed.

Also the Synod of Edinburgh, on 9 April 1684,

> renewed that Article of Perth, ratified in the 1 Act of the Parliament in 1621, anent the confirmation of children; only by that Act the examination is at 8 years old, wheras the Bischop ordains the account they shall give of ther faith, by repeiting the Belieff, Lord's Prayer, and Ten Commandments, and the short Catechisme then used, and the renewing ther baptismall engadgements to be at 16, when they are come to the age of more understanding.[2]

This edict does not seem to have been followed in Edinburgh, and there is no indication that it was revived by any other diocesan synod.

The restoration of the rights of patrons naturally meant that bishops again exercised their right of patronage over certain parishes. The bishop frequently had the right over a substantial number of parishes in his diocese. In the Presbytery of Dunkeld there were twenty-two kirks. The bishop had patronage in seven, the Archbishop of St Andrews in one, local noblemen and lairds in thirteen, and the Crown in one.[3]

On occasions, at least, the bishops took quite seriously the needs and desires of the parish in their appointments. Robert Leighton,

---

[1] *Works*, II, 450.   [2] *Dunkeld*, I, 62, n. 4.   [3] Ibid., II, 116–17.

in a letter to the heritors of the parish of Straton, presented a Mr James Aird as "a person fit for the charge of the ministry now vacant with you . . . [since] it is my duty to present". But "unless you invite him to preach, and after hearing of him, declare your consent and desire towards his embracing of the call you may be secure from the trouble of hearing any further concerning him, either from himself or me".[1]

Leighton, however, was not the only bishop who showed this concern. The Minister of Kilmodan, Mr Fullertoun, had been deprived in 1681 for his failure to take the Test, and the patron, the Bishop of Galloway, had appointed Mr Andrew Fraser. However, on 20 May 1682 Hector Maclean, the Bishop of Argyll, sent a letter to the Bishop of Galloway informing him that Mr Fullertown had now taken the Test, that he was "so very dear to the people of his paroch", and that Mr Fraser had refused the presentation. He urged the Bishop to present Mr Fullertown again to Kilmodan, and this was accordingly done.[2]

Any attempt to estimate fairly the general character of the Restoration bishops must recognize the considerable variety of the Scottish bench. Robert Leighton, Bishop of Dunblane, Commendator of Glasgow, and Archbishop of Glasgow, was the outstanding bishop of the period. His deep piety and nobility of spirit are recognized even by his opponents. Wodrow, who looks upon the Restoration period as the *History of the Sufferings of the Church of Scotland*, wrote a surprisingly accurate description of Leighton.

His character was by far the best of any of the bishops now set up: and to give him his due, he was a man of very considerable learning, an excellent utterance, and of a grave and abstracted

[1] *Works*, II, 462.

[2] *Miscellany of the Scottish History Society*, III, 81. In 1676 the heritors, gentlemen, and elders of Abertarfe and Glenmoriston requested the patrons of their kirk, the Lord Bishop of Moray and the Reverend Mr James Steward, Chancellor of Moray, to appoint Mr Robert Monroe to that "benefice and office . . . seeing wee haue had divers tymes great satisfaction of his doctrine". This request was approved by Murdoch Mackenzie, Bishop of Moray, as well as by the Chancellor. Copies of the documents are recorded in the minutes of Presbytery. *Inverness and Dingwall*, pp. 70–71.

conversation. He was reckoned devout, and an enemy to persecution, and professed a great deal of meekness and humility. By many he was judged void of any doctrinal principle, and his close correspondence with some of his relations at Doway in popish orders, made him suspected as very much indifferent as to all professions, which bear the name of Christian. He was much taken with some of the popish mystic writers, and indeed a latitudinarian, and of an over extensive charity. His writings published since the revolution, evidence his abilities and that he was very much superior to his fellows.[1]

Leighton was the only member of the episcopate who made a serious effort to solve the problem of nonconformity on any basis other than repression. He genuinely sought to overcome the conflicts of his day by real humility and purity of love. His commentaries, meditations, and sermons, as well as his *Rules and Instructions for a Holy Life*, comprise the major devotional contribution of the Scottish episcopate of the Restoration. It is little wonder that the Glasgow Town Council, hearing in 1673 that Leighton was planning to resign, appealed to Lauderdale to prevent the resignation, "considering that the whoill citie and incorporatioune therin hes lived peaceablie and quyetlie since the said Archbishop, his coming to this burgh, throw his Christian cariage and behaveor towards them, and by his government with great discretioune and moderatioune".[2] It is also a commentary on the times to note that Leighton did resign in despair and retire to England, where he died in 1684.

In addition to Leighton, there were a few other prelates who were worthy and noble members of the first estate. Patrick Scougall, Bishop of Aberdeen from 1664 until 1682, reminds one very much of Leighton in his gentle piety and modest but very effective administration of his diocese. Burnet writes:

> [His] endearing gentleness ... to all that differed from him, his great strictness in giving Orders, his most unaffected humility and contempt of the World, were things so singular in him, that they deserved to be much more admired than his other Talents, which were

---

[1] *History*, i, 238.   [2] Butler, *Life*, p. 501.

also extraordinary, a wonderful strength of Judgment, a dexterity in the conduct of Affairs, which he imployed chiefly in the making up of Differences, and a Discretion in his whole deportment.[1]

David Mitchell was a minister of Edinburgh, a Laudian, and a friend of Bishop William Forbes during the reign of Charles I. During the Interregnum he fled to England, and thence to Holland, where "being a good mechanic, he gained his bread by making clocks and watches".[2] He was consecrated Bishop of Aberdeen on 3 June 1663, and he died the following February. He was "a little man, of a brisk lively temper, well learned, and a good preacher. He lived a single life, and his manners were without reproach."[3]

Henry Guthrie, the second Bishop of Dunkeld, is remembered for his *Memoirs*. He had been deposed during the Interregnum, and was voted 150*l. scots* at the Restoration for his sufferings (a sum which he never received). Likewise George Wishart, Bishop of Edinburgh, and a close friend of Montrose, wrote a *History of the War in Scotland, under the conduct of the great Marquis of Montrose,* in "elegant Latin".[4]

Most of the Restoration bishops, however, came from the Resolutioner party and had conformed during the late troubles. George Haliburton, minister of Perth, became Bishop of Dunkeld; Murdoch Mackenzie, minister of Elgin, became Bishop of Moray; Patrick Forbes, minister at Alford, became Bishop of Caithness; John Paterson, minister at Aberdeen, became Bishop of Ross; David Strachan, minister at Fettercairn, became Bishop of Brechin; David Fletcher, minister at Melrose, became Bishop of Argyll; Robert Wallace, minister at Barnwell, became Bishop of the Isles; James Sharp, minister of Crail, became Archbishop of St Andrews; Andrew Fairfowl, minister at Dunse, became Archbishop of Glasgow. All had taken the Covenant.

There is no need to assume that all these men were merely hypocritical in their change of belief. Many may well have felt as did Leighton (who had also subscribed to the Covenant) in

---

[1] *The Life of William Bedell* (1685), Preface.   [2] *Domestic Annals*, II, 297.
[3] Ibid.   [4] Keith, *Historical Catalogue*, p. 63.

E

defending his change: " . . . man is a mutable, changing essence both in body and mind, frequently misinformed, yet acts according to light at the time, so he is still to act the ingenuous part, as God, His Word, and his conscience dictate." [1] Still it was easy to suspect these men of compromising their conscience, and at best it must be said that "All of these were persons of respectable character, but not one among them was remarkable for learning or ability".[2]

The very gross immoralities of which these bishops were accused by some contemporary pamphlets of the time are more of an indication of the attitude of covenanters towards the bishops than of the lives of the prelates themselves.[3]

The Restoration Church was especially unfortunate in the choice of James Sharp, who was Primate from 1662 until his brutal murder in 1679. Actually this was the second attempt to assassinate him, an unsuccessful attempt having been made in 1666. He had been sent to England in 1660 by the Resolutioners to assure the maintenance of a Presbyterian settlement, at least in Scotland. As he failed to achieve this, he was widely regarded by many as a traitor, who sold the Church to episcopacy in exchange for the primacy. His extensive correspondence in 1660 [4] hardly sustains this view. Nevertheless, he was a man of mediocre abilities, and "generally regarded as self-interested".[5] The first sermon that he preached in St Andrews was on the text, "I am determined to know nothing among you, save Jesus Christ, and him crucified". But "his sermon did not run much on the words, but in a discourse vindicating himself, and pressing Episcopacy and the utility of it".[6]

The ever-loquacious Gilbert Burnet, while still the young Minister of Saltoun, presented his opinion of the bishops in "A

---

[1] Knox, *Robert Leighton*, p. 171.
[2] Grub, *An Ecclesiastical History of Scotland*, III, 197–8.
[3] See, for example, *A Brief and True Account of the Sufferings of the Church of Scotland Occasioned by the Episcopalians Since the year 1660.*
[4] Much of this correspondence is printed in Wodrow, *History*, I, Introduction.
[5] Henderson, *Religious Life in Seventeenth-Century Scotland*, p. 175.
[6] *Domestic Annals*, II, 291.

Memorial of diverse grievances and abuses in this Church". His memorial was scarcely flattering:

> Now this excellent government is indeed restored, but alas its not animat wt the ancient spirit. . . . Do you think any desire [this] form of Church government only for its selfe? Sure it will never be sought for upon that ground alone, but as it may be a powerful mean of advancing the great designs of the gospel. What moral virtue or Christian grace is raised to any greater height by yor coming in? . . . Your non-residence would have bin judged scandalous even by the Council of Trent. How often have any of yow visited yor diocies? It is now four year since ye were set up and I doubt if some of yow have visited one Church. . . . Yow are not Bishops yt yow may live at ease and ply the affairs of the State. . . . Some of yow preach scarce ever, others only when yow are at yor own houses.[1]

Burnet goes on to accuse them of using too much persecution and force, of being too pompous and grand, with too many "high places, brave horses, coaches and titles", and of enriching "yourselves with the goods of the Church".[2] Even though some of the statements are clearly exaggerated, yet his accusations may well reflect the opinion of many in 1667.

In the latter part of the period, a small reforming group of bishops with quite different interests emerged. Such men as Atkins of Moray and Galloway, Bruce of Dunkeld, Ramsey of Dunblane, and Drummond of Brechin were interested in a National Synod, a liturgy, canons, and the reduction of royal absolutism. Although such a group would find strong support among the young, reforming clergy of Aberdeen, they were conspicuous only by their failure to modify the settlement, two of them incurring sufficient royal displeasure to suffer deprivation.

[1] *Miscellany of the Scottish History Society*, II, 340–58.

[2] By 1685 his opinion had changed considerably. He wrote: "I shall not add much of the Bishops that have been in that Church since the last re-establishing of the Order, but that I have observed among the few of them, to whom I had the honour to be known particularly, as great, and as exemplary things, as ever I met with in all Ecclesiastical History: Not only the practice of the strictest of all the Antient Canons, but a pitch of Vertue and Piety beyond what can fall under common imitation, or be made the measure of even the most Angelical rank of men. . . . *The Life of William Bedell* (1685), Preface.

It may be possible to look at Scottish episcopacy in perspective if we compare it to the more traditional concept of the episcopate as it has developed throughout the history of the Church. At no point is the discontinuity sharper than in the complete absence of Confirmation. The whole programme of confirmation tours which was so conspicuous a part of the life of a bishop in England had no parallel in Scotland. The bishop in Scotland did hold some visitations of parishes; indeed, he often presided over the more important or difficult visitations. But the larger part of this work was delegated to the presbyteries, and, as in the past, the actual visitation of kirks was mainly their responsibility.

In the ordination of clergy and consecration of bishops, the Scottish episcopate followed more traditional paths. While the presbytery conducted the examination of ordinands, and often joined with the bishop in ordination, yet ordination by the presbytery alone ceased to exist within the Established Church.[1] Bishops were consecrated only by bishops, and the practice of three consecrators was adhered to. Yet even here, it should be noted that bishops ordained men simply to the ministry—the orders of "deacon"[2] and "priest" were not recognized in Scotland at this time.

The frequent pastoral letters of the bishops to the lower courts, the careful supervision of discipline over the clergy, and the regular annual (or semi-annual) synod of clergy at which the bishop presided are all in the best tradition of the episcopate. Especially noteworthy is the very real sharing of authority between the bishops and the lower clergy. "The Bishop, with consent of the brethren of synod . . ." is a clause repeated in every synod record. Though the bishop did have an absolute veto over synod actions, and though his authority over individual clergymen was considerable, yet the phrase "bishop and synod" is not simply a formality. The impression which the synod records convey is one

---

[1] See below, p. 96.
[2] The "deacons" mentioned frequently in kirk-session records are lay members of the session, and not one of the orders of the ministry. See below, p. 61 f. For the clerical order of "deacons", see below, p. 97 f.

of real co-operation—a mutual exercise of authority which again is in the best tradition of the episcopate.

The bishops in Scotland, in other words, represent a unique development of the episcopate, although in certain important respects they continued in the usual Western tradition of the Catholic bishop.[1]

[1] See below, p. 88, n. 1.

4

THE COURTS OF THE KIRK

THE Restoration Parliament in 1661 announced that "his majestie . . . doth allow the present administration by sessions, presbetries and synods (they keeping within bounds and behaveing themselffs as said is)".[1] On 2 January 1662 a royal letter forbade these courts to meet without episcopal approval, but such approval was universally given,[2] and thereafter Church courts (with the exception of the General Assembly) met regularly throughout the reign.

The three courts constituted an ascending scale of jurisdiction: kirk-sessions were limited to the local parish, presbyteries exercised jurisdiction over a small group of parishes, while synods included several presbyteries and were synonymous with a diocese.

The exercise of ecclesiastical discipline was a major duty of these judicatories. Such discipline was a characteristic feature of Calvinism during and after the Reformation. Based upon a doctrine of the sovereignty and holiness of God, of the autonomous authority of the Church to administer discipline, and of the necessity of ordering all life by what was believed to be the injunctions of Holy Scripture, a whole system of discipline (of which Sabbatarianism was a most conspicuous element) was administered by a series of courts that received accusations, tried cases, and decreed sentences.[3] Apart from discipline, much of the ordinary day-by-day business of the Church was also handled by these courts.

---

[1] *Source Book of Scottish History*, III, 156.
[2] Charles's instructions in 1670 required that such approval be given. The letter is printed in Stephen, *Life of Sharp*, pp. 430–4.
[3] McNeill, *The History and Character of Calvinism*, pp. 138, 188–9.

KIRK-SESSIONS

It was the responsibility of the kirk-session to administer the local affairs of the parish, to care for the poor, to assist with other public projects, to supervise the discipline of those within its bounds, and to pass on to the presbytery those cases which it could not handle. The Synod of St Andrews authorized kirk-sessions as follows:

> My Lord Archbishop, with the Synod, considering how necessary it is that ministers be assisted in exercise of disciplin within their respectiv congregations, [do appoint that in every congregation] the several ministers shal assume and choos a competent number of fitt persons, according to the bounds of [the] parish, to oversee the maners of the peopl, to assist in Session for bearing doun of profanity and disorder, and advancing of good order in the congregation, and also for taking care of the collections for the poor, and distributing what is colected for their necessities.[1]

The Synod of Aberdeen avoided the use of the term "session", but otherwise reconstituted the lowest court as it had formerly been.

> It is enacted by the Bishope, with consent of the brethren of the Synod, that every minister within this diocie shall mak choice of so many within his paroch of the most able, qualified, and understanding persons, to have ane inspectione and oversight of the people, and observe their wayes of walking, and that they shall delate to the minister scandalous walkers, that they may be censured according to the approven Actis of the Church, and that they concurr with and assist the minister to the effect foresaid.[2]

The session consisted of the minister, who would preside, and the elected elders and deacons. Meetings were usually held weekly, though the day of meeting varied. The Session of Banff met on Sunday,[3] while the Session of Elgin normally met on a weekday.[4] Although synodical legislation gave authority to the minister to select the members of his session, it was more common for the

---

[1] *Dunkeld*, I, 314.
[2] *Alford*, p. 3.
[3] *Banff*, II, 44–5.
[4] *Elgin*, II, 302.

session to elect its own members. Thus we find in the Register of
the Kirk-Session of Rattray the following:

> March 11, 1666—Quo die, the Session takeing to consideratione
> that severall of the eldership who sat formerlie are deceist, and others
> left their charge, quherfor they resolve to admitt James Zeaman of
> Eastwalkmiln, Harie Crokat in Westmiln, and George Thomsone in
> Midledrimie, to be members of the Sessione, quhilk is to be intimat
> the nixt Lord's day.[1]

Deacons were also chosen by the session and seem to have been
members of that body as well as the elders. Thus in 1685 the Kirk-
Session of Rattray ordered:

> In regard that there was but one member of Session in the upper
> part of the paroch, the Session thought it convenient that one at
> least should for the present be added to their number, and con-
> descended upon David Atkine as a fitt person to be admitted
> Deacon.[2]

The same minute gives an interesting account of the duties of
the deacon:

> David Atkine was . . . admitted unto the office of a deacon in
> the Church: at which time, the minister exhorted him to take inspec-
> tion of the needs of the poor, to gather the charity of the people faith-
> fully, to give a good example by his own life and conversation, and
> to take care that scandals be not concealed: all which he promised
> by the Grace of God to do.[3]

Of course, such deacons were in no sense an order of the
ministry. They had no examinations; they were not licensed by
the bishop, nor did they assist in conducting the ordinary Sunday
worship of the congregation.[4]

There is no evidence that elders and deacons were elected by a
vote of the congregation, and they were admitted to their office
at a public meeting of the session, not at a public service of the
church.

Sometimes it was not easy to persuade men to accept election

---

[1] *Dunkeld*, II, 84.   [2] Ibid., p. 87.   [3] Ibid.
[4] For deacons as an order of the ministry, see below, p. 97 f.

as elders. In 1684 a Royal letter was issued charging them to accept election within fifteen days under penalty of rebellion.

> This arose upon a complaint made to the Bischop of Edinburgh by sundry of his Ministers, that the gentry refused to concurre with them, so that they ather could get no Session constitute at all, or else it was only of the tenandry.[1]

Kirk-sessions frequently dealt with matters affecting the administration of the local parish. On 22 September the Session of Elgin gave permission to Mr William Annand to bury his grandmother beside her husband in the choir of the church, but "with this provision that no more graves be make in that quire at any tyme hereafter".[2] On 2 May 1680 the Kirk-Session of Banff ordered the "old gilded chalice" to be made "into two cups [for] the Sacrament of the Lord's Supper . . . providing always that the same arms of the anonymous donour, which the old chalice bore, should be upon the new cups, and the town's arms also".[3] In 1681 the same session laid a tax of 179*l*. 3*s*. *scots* upon the "heritors for repairing the fabric of the kirk", while in the same year "Patrick Reid, church officiar, [was] challenged for not ringing the bell daily at five in the morning and at nine at night".[4] On 11 December 1687 the minister reported to the Session of Banff that Archbishop Sharp had given 1000 marks to the town of Banff for the poor. He had now been dead eight years, but the 1000 marks had been withheld by his son, Sir William Sharp. "The Session resolve to write to Sir William, and if he deliver it not up speedily they will pursue him legally."[5] On 2 September 1666 the Kirk-Session of Aberdeen ordered that John Kilgour should receive all collections from marriages and baptisms "and that for his ringing the nyn hour bell at night",[6] while on 20 February 1681 we find the following minute of that session:

> It was intimate this day that from this tyme forth non should bring along dogs wt them to the Church by reason the public worship was

---

1 Fountainhall's *Historical Notices*, II, 537; *Dunkeld*, II, 85.
2 *Elgin*, II, 302.   3 *Banff*, II, 56.
4 Ibid.   5 Ibid., pp. 57–8.
6 *Records of Old Aberdeen*, II, 63.

so much disturbed by the noise occasioned by them every sabbath day.

The sd. day it was ordered by the Minister and Session that to prevent any noise by dogs Georg Donald in this toune should haue ane groat out of the Collection every Sabbath for to hold them out of the Church.[1]

One of the main functions of the session was the supervision of the discipline of the parish. Difficult cases, as well as those involving more than one parish, were handled by the presbytery, which meant that most of the cases would appear before that body. However, the kirk-sessions themselves dealt with a surprisingly large number of cases.

Attendance at church was required on Sunday, and the elders searched the town for those who were absent. On 29 July 1666 the elders of the Session of Aberdeen reported that they were having difficulty in fulfilling this duty:

The sd. day there was a regrait giuen in by those who searched the toune on the Sabbath efternoone in tyme of sermone that some houses in the toune did hold their doores fast and would not giue them libertie to searche there houses: Quvpon it is oerdained that intimatione be made the next Lords day that these who closes their doors against these elders that searcheth for the tyme shall be holden as guiltie persones and shall be punished accordinglie.[2]

On 28 March 1675 it was reported to the same session "that men and boys uswally playit kits in the snow kirkyard and Dowglad wind in tyme of sermon the officer ordered to goe their the next sabbath".[3] On 7 November 1680 this session discovered that "there was seen some servant men & boys belonging to Wm. Gray & others about the b. of Don playing at the golfe in the links beyond the bridge in tyme of the afternoons sermon the officer ordered to try for account of ther names & to cite them and ther masters to the next session".[4] On 22 April 1688 "ane great compleant was given in this day against Alexr Crystel wright for fastening the door of the trades loft with garron nails and double

[1] *Records of Old Aberdeen*, II, 74. [2] Ibid., p. 63.
[3] Ibid., p. 68. [4] Ibid., p. 73.

trees so that non of the trades men could have access to sit in it to hear the Word of God".[1] On 21 January 1673 the Session of Elgin "delait John Lambe and Alexander Mansone for break of Sabath in playing at the cards against the Lords day".[2] On 26 January 1664 Elspet Redhead was accused of "calling George Duncan in Pluscarden a theife",[3] while the following April Margaret Tamsone was accused of charming "and being gravlie spokine to be the bischope [who was also the Minister of Elgin] she confessed that she haid charmed sundrie children and men".[4] The Session of Banff considered the case of Alexander Neill and two others who were accused of "shearing on the preceeding fast-day", while Christian Mortimer was found guilty of bringing in peats on a fast-day and reviling the elders who challenged her. Margaret Wilsone was accused of going to a "superstitious well", while Janet Sherrae was accused of "lewd conversation".[5] Mr Arthur Gordon was charged with being "married by a priest wt a papist woman".[6] Cases of charming were regarded as so serious that they were frequently referred to the presbytery. The Session of Aberdeen referred Jean Nimbrie and Helen Collie, who were accused of charming, to the presbytery, declaring that "the Minister and Session would not do anything with them".[7]

The nature of such charming is well illustrated by this last case. The Session record for 5 June 1681 stated that

> Jean Nimbrie . . . confessed that she cured the sd. Helen Collie by a charm . . . [and went on to] declaire the maner how she charmed her, she sd. it was by taking a hose and tying a threed about it, then putting the hose about the sd. Helen she used these words, the Lord Jesus Chryst, by the sea rode, and the fevers on his syde and buried them in a grave, in the name of the Father, Sone and Holy Ghost.[8]

---

[1] *Records of Old Aberdeen*, II, 87.   [2] *Elgin*, II, 309.
[3] Ibid., p. 302.   [4] Ibid., p. 303.
[5] *Banff*, II, 47–8.
[6] *Records of Old Aberdeen*, II, 59.
[7] Ibid., p. 75. Similarly, Isobell Cuming, accused by the Session of Elgin for charming, was "referred to the presbytrie". *Elgin*, II, 299.
[8] Ibid.

Examples of such cases of discipline could be multiplied at great length. The Session of Aberdeen usually dealt with fifteen or twenty at each meeting. Not all of these were new cases, however, many being carried over from meeting to meeting.

Those who were found guilty by the session were given various punishments. The most common punishments used by the session were admonishment from the pulpit, fines, and penance *in sacco* on the pillar. There are many examples of the use of each.

On 15 November 1675 the Session of Banff tried Margaret Spence, who was

> seen casting water seven tymes out the sea toward the toun, and five stones into the sea, in time of morning prayer the preceding Sabbath. She deponed upon her soul's salvation she did for preventing the feavere and not out of any principle of magick, adding that of negliegence and not of intention she cast the water toward the town. To be rebuked before the pulpit.[1]

The standard fine for fornication in Banff was 4*l. scots*,[2] while the Session of Elgin adopted a list of fines on 17 January 1665. The penalty for each fornication was six marks for the man and four for the woman, while "for ilk adulterie at leist sexteine punds and mor according to the abilitie of the transgressors and discretione of the sessione".[3]

One of the most common sentences was that of exposure on the stool or on the pillar, usually in sackcloth. This was a high stool or bench placed in a conspicuous part of the church, usually near the pulpit. Those to be punished in this way were required to sit (sometimes stand) upon this stool during the Sunday service. On 10 January 1664 the Session of Banff discovered "that the pillar and persons therein standing is not conspicuous enough, the heighting of it was referred to the treasurer", and on 7 March it was "found the pillar of repentance is erected of new".[4] On 4 April 1669 the Session of Aberdeen "enacted and ordained . . . that non remove off the penitentiall seat untill the blessing be pronounced by the minr, [otherwise] . . . it shall not serve them

---

[1] *Banff*, II, 50.   [2] Ibid., p. 48.
[3] *Elgin*, II, 304.   [4] *Banff*, II, 44.

for a dayes appearance",[1] while on 17 July 1681 the session made
a further attempt to ensure the decent behaviour of penitents:

> It was complained upon this day that the faultors does not behaue
> themselves as they ought to do, qrupon it is appointed that the
> officer take the plaids from the women as they goe up to the pillar,
> & that non of them sit ther with any thing about them except those
> that weares the habite, also that they . . . faces to the Minister.[2]

Penitents were either sentenced to a definite number of appearances on the pillar or were simply to continue to suffer this
penalty until they showed signs of repentance. On 10 April 1664
the Session of Banff tried Elspet Faitch "for cursing and slandering
her neighbours. [She] is ordained to appear before the pulpit on
the Lord's day in sackcloth till she shows evidences of repentance".[3]
Three years later she was again before the session and convicted
of superstitious practices:

> August 11.—Compeared Elspet Faitch, Issobel Watson, and Helen
> Milne, who confessed their going to the wall [well] of grace beyond
> Spey; ordained to stand in sackcloth upon the publick place of
> repentance barefooted and each to pay 40s.[4]

Sometimes the sentence involved a thorough humiliation of the
offender. On 15 July 1666 the Session of Aberdeen dealt with the
case of two women and a man who were guilty of scandalous
behaviour. The session

> ordained that the saids Margt. Milne and Barbara Dune shall be
> put in the Goves and stand therin betwixt the 2d and 3d. bell and
> the sd. Alext Sangster to be put in the stocks at the kirk stylle that
> same tyme and after the 3d bell they are to goe to the pillar and after
> sermon they are to appeare before the pulpit in sackcloth and be
> publicklie rebuiked for all their forsd. scandalous carages.[5]

On the other hand, the same session could show leniency and
consideration toward a pregnant girl who was a first offender:

> 12 April, 1688—The sd. day . . . ane supplication from Jonnet
> Georg desyring that the sessione would indulge her with that favour

[1] *Records of Old Aberdeen*, ii, 66.   [2] Ibid., p. 75.
[3] *Banff*, ii, 44.   [4] Ibid., p. 47.
[5] *Records of Old Aberdeen*, ii, 62–3.

not to appear in publick before the congregatione but that she may have libertie to acknowledge hir miscariage before the session in regaird it was her first fault, and next that she was verie bigg wt chyld . . . q'vpon the sessione taking her case to consideratione ordained her to appeare the next day before the sessione and acknowledge her trespesse and to pay 40 shilling scots of penaltie the sd. day.[1]

One other form of punishment which was occasionally used was the jougs. This was a short chain, one end of which was attached to the wall of the church and the other to a ring fastened around the offender's neck.[2] The Session of Banff found use for them on one occasion :

July 26, 1673—Patrick Moorison and his wife for their scandalous carriage to one another are enjoyned the following Sabbath *in sacco* to stand in joggs betwixt the second and third bell then incontinentlie to betake themselves to the public stool of repentance and with open voice befor the whole congregation acknowledge ther offensive behaviour, with certificate they will be banished the town as vagabonds if they do the like again.[3]

Close co-operation between the kirk-sessions and the civil magistrates was also typical of the period. A visiting Englishman wrote of the presence of magistrates at the Session:

In these Meetings the Provost or some other Civil Magistrate was present to give 'em Countenance, inforce their Acts, and awe Sawcy Offenders, which as it took off much of the *Odium* the Church had otherwise had, so it made her Censures more terrible upon instances of Scandal.[4]

Although the attendance of the magistrates was not very common at kirk-sessions, yet the keepers of the keys of the Kingdom worked closely with the keepers of the keys of the town prison. Thus the Session of Banff in 1671 dealt with the case of John Smith, a married man, who was accused of being the father of Margaret Philip's child. He denied the charge. "The Session thought fitt

---

[1] *Records of Old Aberdeen*, II, 64–5.
[2] There is a drawing of the jougs at Duddingston Church in *Domestic Annals*, II, 501.
[3] *Banff*, II, 49.   [4] Morer, *Short Account*, pp. 47–8.

that he should be incarcerate until he should sett suretie als oft as he was called, and that it would be ane mean to bring him to ane confession." [1] He was put in prison and confessed. Three years earlier the same session had committed three persons to prison [2] "for agravated breach of the seventh commandment".[3]

The session was also responsible for the poor of the parish, for the support of general charitable movements recommended by higher courts, and for the support of numerous public projects. On 4 April 1669 the Session of Elgin collected 66*l.* 4*s.* 10*d.* for the "distressed widowes of Brough [when] . . . ther men wes lost be sea".[4] On 4 November 1688 the Session of Banff took steps to reform the local hospital.

> It being represented that the hospital, founded and doted by the Lord Banff's grandfather, had not its due number of men, and that those in it had not their allowance of meat and cloath, but were in a starving condition and begging charity from the session, it was agreed on that Baillie Fyfe should be commissioned to speak to the Lord Banff, both to fill up the number of men, and to supply them according to the will of the mortification, that they getting what is due may not be burdensome to the town.[5]

Finally, testimonials, which were needed by those who planned to move to another parish, were issued by the minister and session. In January 1665 the Session of Elgin fixed a fee "for ilk testimoniall directed without the paroch [of] sex schiling . . . except servants whose testimoniall sould be free".[6] These testimonials were proof of uncensorable behaviour, and a stranger who arrived in a parish without one was regarded with great suspicion. The Session of Banff (1664) recorded an "Intimation made from the

---

[1] *Banff*, II, 48.
[2] Ibid., p. 44.
[3] Other sessions also found the alignment with local civil authorities of great value. In 1675 the "bischope with the session of Elgin [the bishop being the Minister of Elgin] judges Christane Troup worthie of banischment from this corporation for her fornication and adultery and intreats the magistrats of this burge to interpone their authoritie for her banishment. She is ordained to ward till the magistrats consent to the censure." Apparently the magistrates did consent, for Christane Troup's name does not appear again in the session records. *Elgin*, II, 310.
[4] *Elgin*, II, 306.   [5] *Banff*, II, 58.   [6] *Elgin*, II, 304.

pulpit that non recept Marjory Bisset, till she bring a certificate from Aberdeen".[1]

PRESBYTERIES

The weekly meetings of kirk-sessions were invaluable in the maintenance of that ideal of disciplined morality which was so conspicuous a part of Scottish reformed tradition. However, the jurisdiction of a session was limited to one parish and its authority dependent upon the co-operation of the local elders. For this reason, the kirk-sessions were overshadowed by the presbyteries, and the latter courts became more important units in the administrative and disciplinary structure of the Church. In the regular meetings of the presbyteries a vast amount of the ordinary discipline and administration of the Church was handled.

Presbyteries were not part of the Knoxian reformation. One of the ancestors of the presbytery in Scotland was a meeting known as the "Exercise". This was a group of clergy (usually laity were present also) who met at regular intervals to hear a commentary or "exercise" on a text of Scripture. This was followed by a second commentary or "addition"—hence the practice of "exercising and adding". The custom was recommended by John Knox in the *First Book of Discipline* (1560) and continued throughout the sixteenth and seventeenth centuries. After the *Second Book of Discipline* (1581) presbyteries began to develop specifically as disciplinary and administrative assemblies. By 1590 presbyteries had been established in most of Scotland. It was also in the latter part of the sixteenth century that the presbytery and the exercise began to unite and fulfil both functions as one body. In 1579 the General Assembly ordered that "the exercise may be judged a presbytery".[2]

During the Restoration the terms "presbytery" and "exercise" were used interchangeably to refer to the second court of the Church of Scotland. There was a tendency in the north to

[1] *Banff*, II, 45.
[2] G. D. Henderson, "The Exercise", *Records of the Scottish Church History Society*, VII, 24. The article contains a valuable summary of the whole development.

prefer the earlier term "exercise".[1] However, even here the term "presbytery" was sometimes used. The preference for "exercise" probably reflected the dislike for a purely presbyterian settlement which was especially strong north of the Tay.

Presbyteries were established with much the same boundaries as they had had under James VI and Charles I. In October 1662 it was

. . . enacted and ordered by the Bischope, [of Aberdeen] with consent of the brethren of the Synod, that the meitings of the brethren of the Exercises shall be at the same places wher they did meet for exercise in the tyme of Bishopes.[2]

For the most part this instruction involved very little discontinuity with the past. The Presbytery of Elgin continued to meet after 1662 much as it had in the past, as did the Presbyteries of Inverness, Dingwall, Fordyce, and Dunkeld (though a Protestor Presbytery had developed here, and was absorbed at the time of the Restoration).[3]

In 1662 the Synod of St Andrews gave the following directions for the constitution of presbyteries:

. . . there shal be, [within] the same several precincts within the Dioces that formerly wer, meetings of the ministers of those respective bounds for the exercise of their gifts as formerly, for putting to tryal young men who offer themselves to be probationers, for trying the gifts and abilities of such as are presented to churches, their presentations being transmitted to the several meetings by the Lord Archbishop, for trying and examining scandals referred to them by particular Sessions, and proceeding toward the censur of the same: only that no sentences of excommunication against any person be pronounced, nor sentenc of suspension nor deposition against any minister, without acquainting the Ordinar, and having his authority to it.[4]

---

[1] For example, *The Records of the Exercise of Alford.*   [2] *Alford*, p. 3.

[3] The records of the presbyteries which are available show clearly that they met regularly after October 1662, and do not substantiate Wodrow's statement that "all church judicatories . . . are pulled down, to make way for the episcopal throne. It was some years after this [1662] before the curates and inferior clergy in most places were allowed to meet for the exercise of their gifts together." *History*, 1, 262.   [4] *Dunkeld*, 1, 314.

F

Actually the list is by no means complete, and the presbyteries were frequently involved in more activities than this list would imply.

One of the few changes made at the Restoration was the exclusion of the elders of the session, or ruling elders, from presbytery meetings. There is some disagreement as to the reason. Probably, it was to reduce the power of a lay element which was not nearly so amenable to episcopal control as were licensed preachers (or expectants) [1] and ministers. In any case, the presbytery was comprised of only those ministers of parishes and licensed preachers who lived within the bounds of the presbytery.

Meetings were usually held monthly, though in the summer they were sometimes increased to every three weeks.[2] The difficulty of travel, as well as the severity of Scottish winters, is often reflected in presbytery minutes. On 8 April 1674 the Presbytery of Alford recorded that there had been no meeting since December "in respect the brethren could not travell neither on horse nor foot, through the greatnes of the storme".[3]

Moderators of presbytery were no longer elected by the brethren, but were appointed by the bishop. Usually they were appointed for a definite period, either six months or a year, although reappointment for another term was common. Frequently they were appointed by the bishop and synod acting together. In 1664 the Synod of Aberdeen ordered "all moderators of Exercises . . . continued",[4] and the Synod of Dunblane frequently appointed moderators "by vote of the Bishop and Synod".[5] In 1666 the Synod of Aberdeen ordered the appointment of vice-moderators to act in the absence of the moderator,[6] while in 1676 the synod ordered that in the absence of the moderator and vice-moderator, the rest of the brethren (if there were a quorum) should choose one of their number to moderate *pro temporo*.[7]

One of the main duties of a minister was faithful attendance at meetings of the presbytery, and numerous attempts were made by

[1] See below, pp. 93 ff.
[2] This was the regular pattern of the Presbytery of Alford during the decade 1662–71.
[3] *Alford*, p. 209.   [4] Ibid., p. 59.
[5] *Dunkeld*, II, 5.   [6] *Alford*, p. 81.   [7] Ibid., p. 268.

that body to ensure that the members be present and on time. The Presbytery of Dunfermline ordered in April 1664 that "If any brother be absent from the Presbytrie tuo days, without a lauful excuse, his name is to be given in to the Synod", while in October 1685 the Synod of St Andrews ordered that

> If any prisbiter absent himselffe from the meeteing of the Exercise, or from the Synod, without a dispensation from the Archbishop, or a lawfull escuse . . . for his absence from the meeteing of the Exercise, he shall pay a rix dollor, and for his absence from the Synod twentie merkes Scots money, besid a publick rebook for the first tyme; and if he be found twice guiltie of same fault, he shall be suspended.[1]

Similar action can be found in almost all the existing synod or presbytery records. Members were also expected to be on time, and were rebuked or fined for tardiness. On 13 October 1663 the Presbytery of Dingwall decided that "everie broyr cuming late should give in a sex pens to be given to the poore, [but] Mrs Donald Rosse, Robt Rosse, George Cumin who came behind tyme today being desyred to pay, refused".[2] The rest of the session was spent arguing about this momentous decision, and it was finally decided to "refer the mater to the Bishop's determinaon". The Presbytery of Alford did not find this so controversial an issue. On 24 August 1664, "by unanimous consent of the brethren, it is ordained that the meittings of the Exercise bee kept punctually bee two hours, and whosoever shall transgresse the said ordinance shall pay a shilling".[3]

Attendance at presbytery was not easy. It often meant a long trip by horseback over very rough country. For some men this was a journey of twenty-five, fifty, or even seventy miles. It is not surprising that excuses sometimes arrived instead of members. In 1671 the Minister of Dores could not attend because his horse had been stolen, and in 1675 the Minister of Boleskine was at last preparing his parish for a celebration of the Lord's Supper and could not attend.[4] Such excuses were not automatically accepted,

---

[1] *Dunkeld*, ii, 30–1.   [2] *Inverness and Dingwall*, p. 304.
[3] *Alford*, p. 49.   [4] *Inverness and Dingwall*, p. xxvi.

and ministers whose excuses were judged inadequate could expect censure. On 6 April 1676 the Presbytery of Alford "not finding clearnes anent the relevancie of his [the Minister of Cabrach] excuse" reported the matter to the bishop and synod.[1] The excuse of Mr Hugh Fraser, Minister of Croy in 1674, that he had been on some private business in Aberdeen was not acceptable to the Presbytery of Inverness, and he was "rebuked for his preferreing his privat to this publict concernement".[2]

Considering the difficulty of travel and the amount of time involved, it is amazing that presbyteries could have been held in such a regular manner or so well attended.

The meeting of presbytery was usually opened by calling on the Name of God. This was followed by an exercise and addition, with evaluation of both. Sometimes the exercise and addition were given by the same person, sometimes by two different men.[3] Usually the exercise was "approven", but commendation was not invariable. On 5 September 1667 the Exercise of Alford reported that "Mr James Ross exercised on Romans 15. 23, the doctrin is censured, and hee exhorted to studie more clearnes in his doctrin",[4] and on 3 November 1675 Mr John Irvine, who was not very popular with the presbytery, "exercised on 1 Corinthians 1. 7, and being removed was censured for some incoherencies in his discourse, and when called in, was gravelie admonished to be more methodicall heirafter, that the Exercise and Addition might appear distinct".[5]

On less frequent occasions, the exercise would be followed by a Commonhead. This was a theological discussion on an assigned topic, usually given in Latin. Such topics as: *De Causis secessonis Ecclesiae Reformatae ab Ecclesia Romana, De perfectione et perspeicuitate Scripturae, De transubstantiatione, De peccato originali, De creatione hominis, De universali redemptione* were assigned.[6] The practice seems to have been dying out, except as a part of the trial of

---

[1] *Alford*, p. 260.
[3] Ibid., p. 39; *Alford*, p. 9.
[5] Ibid., p. 256.
[6] *Dunkeld*, II, 28; *Inverness and Dingwall*, p. xxviii.

[2] *Inverness and Dingwall*, p. 47.
[4] *Alford*, p. 100.

candidates. Thus the Presbytery of Meigle held a Commonhead on occasion during the first years of the Restoration, but none was heard after 1671. Although the Synod of Aberdeen (1664) ordered that "the handling of commone heads of controversie be frequently performed by the brethren of the several Exercises, especiallie wher Poprie is most preached",[1] they were not very common in the Exercise of Alford except when a candidate was undergoing trials.

Another pre-Restoration practice continued by the presbyteries was the privy censure. This was a semi-annual or annual examination of the life, doctrine, and faithful discharge of duty of each member of presbytery, he being removed from the meeting during the examination. Usually the privy censure was held just before the meeting of the diocesan synod. There is some evidence that the privy censure had become something of a formality, and attempts were made by both Leighton and Scougall to make it a more effective means of serious examination and reform. In April 1667 Leighton spoke to the Synod of Dunblane about the "bussiness of privy tryalls (as they are called) of ministers in their Presbyteries towards the tyme of the Synod, in which I have perceived in some places (if I may be pardoned that frie word) very much of superficiall empty forme . . .". He went on to propose a series of very searching questions which envisaged a high ideal of pastoral and ministerial life. He then concluded by reminding them of the limitations of public examination of such matters:

> The maine intent in these [questions] . . . is serious reflexion, and that each of us may be stirred up to ask ourselves over againe those and more of the lyke questiones in our most privatt tryalles and our secret scrutinies of our owne heartes and lives, and may redouble our diligence in purgeing ourselves that wee may be in the house of God vesselles of honour, sanctified and meet for the Master's use, and prepared to every good work.[2]

Bishop Scougall did much the same thing in Aberdeen. On 21 April 1675 the Synod of Aberdeen set forth an "Order for

---

[1] *Alford*, p. 59.   [2] *Works*, II, 440–45.

the privat tryall and censure of ministers in their respective Presbytries [that they may] . . . excite one another to faithfulness, zeal and diligence". The next synod meeting in October reported that the Order for Private Censure was most effective for "begitting and mantaining on their hearts a fresh sense of the duties of their calling", and recommended that a sermon on their duties also be preached on the day of privy censure. The Bishop and Synod agreed to the recommendation, but cautiously added "that the sermon hinder not the rest of the work, it is ordered that it doe not exceed half ane hour".[1]

The presbyteries were responsible for a variety of duties. They arranged for the temporary supply of a parish during the vacancy between ministers. Usually one of the members of the presbytery was commissioned to hold such services. The Exercise of Alford ordered, on 20 November 1662:

> In rehard of the decrepit old age of Mr. Andrew Kerre, minister of Glenbuchet, it is ordained that Mr. John Walker go thither on Lord's day, and supplie the charge befor the nixt meitting; as likwise, in respect of the vacancie of Touch, it is ordained that Mr. William Glasse supplie that charge one day befor the nixt meeiting.[2]

Such temporary supply was never very satisfactory and sometimes the presbytery took further responsibility. On 23 April 1663 the Exercise of Alford ordered

> The moderator, Mr. George Garden, Mr. Walter Ritchie, and Mr. James Gordoune . . . to waith upon the Earll of Marre [patron of the Church of Strathdoun] and to entreat his Lordship to present a qualified minister, on account of the urgent necessitie of that people.[3]

On 21 July 1663 the Minister of Dingwall reported that he could not "get the tounes men moved to build the kirk yard dyk". The baillies were summoned before presbytery on 11 August, and again on 1 September. Finally on 22 September the baillies reported that the town council was "content to build the

---

[1] *Alford*, pp. 238–9, 253–4.   [2] Ibid., p. 8.   [3] Ibid., p. 13.

Kirkyard dyk March nixt (considering they could not doe it sooner be reason of the season of the year)".[1]

Presbyteries were responsible also for the examination of the session books of each kirk.[2] They supervised the appraisal of a manse, though only on warrant from their bishop. An accurate appraisal of the manse had serious financial consequences for the minister [3] and was administered with great care by the presbytery. On the day appointed, the presbytery met at the manse, examined the workmen who were to make the appraisal, "took their oaths to do the work in honesty and good conscience, and received their sworn statement of the appraisal".[4]

One of the most important duties of a presbytery was its visitation of those kirks within its bounds. Visitation by a presbytery was much more frequent than visitation by a bishop. Presbytery did not go on a visitation tour, but visited individual kirks at appointed times. Usually visitations took place in the summer months when travel was easiest. Sometimes these visitations were held under warrant from the bishop. The Presbytery of Dunkeld on 1 February 1682 reported that "the Bishop had ordered a visitation to be holden att Weem, and impowered and given commissione to the Moderator and brethren for that effect".[5] More frequently the presbyteries were given a general recommendation to be faithful in their visitations. On 24 April 1674 the Synod of Aberdeen

> ordered that Presbytries be diligent in going about visitationes of those kirks within their boundes, and to beginne at those kirks whose ministers are most frequentlie absent from the Presbyteriall meetings.[6]

Visitations followed a fairly definite pattern. Announcement of the intended visitation would be given well in advance to the parish and minister, and on the day appointed the members of presbytery would meet in the kirk. Often the visitation would be

---

[1] *Inverness and Dingwall*, p. 303.
[2] *Alford*, p. 74.
[3] See below, pp. 110 ff.
[4] *Dunkeld*, 1, 467–8.
[5] Ibid., p. 440.
[6] *Alford*, p. 213.

opened with a sermon. After oath, the elders and heritors would be examined individually about the life and duties of the minister. The minister in turn would be examined about the care with which the elders and heritors had fulfilled their responsibilities. All would be questioned about the minister's stipend, glebe land, manse, the communion vessels and other ecclesiastical furniture, the school and the qualifications of the schoolmaster, the kirk officer, the state of the poor-box, and any other matters pertaining to the life and well-being of the parish.[1]

These visitations could be most effective. On 8 March 1671 Mr James Smith, Minister of Doores, reported to the Presbytery of Inverness that he was having much trouble with his "herd-hearted Parishoners [who did not] concur . . . with him for curbing and suppressing of sin and vice abounding amongst many of his people", and who did not pay him the accustomed stipend. It was decided to hold a visitation at Doores on 29 March, at which time the heritors and elders were told it was "a signe of a gasping devotion among ym, when they wer so close-handed" as to withhold the stipend, and they were severely reprimanded for this and other faults. "Whereupon, ye elders and gentlemen yn present promised to doe him duty herein, and yt yr should not be reason in any tyme coming for the like complent."[2]

In 1675 the Synod of Aberdeen set forth a "Direction for the Visitation of Churches", which followed the usual pattern, but also contained many detailed questions about the life of the minister, the elders, heritors, church fabric, school and school-master, existence of nonconformity, and general state of the parish life.[3]

Regular visitations counted for a great deal in the good ordering of the life of the Church of Scotland. On 15 March 1666, during a visitation of Elgin, it was noted that "for want of accommodatione manie are deprived of the benefit of the word. It was recommended to see to the better accommodation of the people

---

[1] Those visitation records which have survived are a most valuable source of knowledge of the parish life of the time. See *Banff*, II, 53–4; *Elgin*, II, 371, 377; *Dunkeld*, II, 133–5; *Inverness and Dingwall*, pp. 13–14, 18, 29.
[2] *Inverness and Dingwall*, pp. 8–10.   [3] *Alford*, pp. 231 ff.

by the erection of the new church." By October 1669 the new church was complete and services were held in it for the first time.[1]

To the average members of a kirk, the visitation of the presbytery was the chief visible sign of an ecclesiastical power and authority above that of the local parish. Both they and their minister were judged by the authority of this presbytery. While it could technically be claimed that presbyteries were acting as agents of the bishop, since they met only on his approbation, this subordination would hardly be obvious to the average parishioner. He saw the members of the presbytery ride into town on the day they had appointed—the presbytery held court and the presbytery administered rebukes or noted its approval. For such laymen the presbytery was an important, integral part of their church life, while the bishop must have seemed to many a distant and somewhat irrelevant figure.

The most important single duty of the presbyteries and the one which occupied most of their time was the administration of discipline. Their responsibilities were similar to those of the kirk-sessions, but the cases handled were usually of a more serious nature, or involved delinquents who would not submit to the discipline of the session.

Adultery was a frequent problem in these rough times. This was specifically recognized by the Exercise of Alford, which, on 12 August 1668, "taking to their consideration the frequencie of rape, and particularly within the bounds of this Presbiterie, how that many were accessorie to the violent taking away of women, and either forceing them to follie or to marriage, thought fit to referr the same to the Synod . . . .".[2] However, the presbytery often handled the actual cases in a most effective manner. On 2 July 1684 the Presbytery of Inverness ordered the following method of dealing with a case of doubtful paternity:

> Donald Bain, suspected Adultere wt ye sd Agnes Makenzie, continewing in his denyall is ordained to purge himselfe by his oath befor ye Congregation of Inverness, wt his hand on ye childs head,

---

[1] *Elgin*, II, 371, 307.   [2] *Alford*, p. 123.

and in presence of ye forsd Agnes, and yet ye Ministers are apointed to be at pains wt him to see if it be possible to bring him to any acknowledgment.[1]

To require the suspected father to take an oath on the head of the child was not uncommon. In 1677 it was described as "the practise of this Kirk and Kingdome".[2] Those who tried to escape the discipline of the presbytery were pursued relentlessly. In all the parishes of Alford, notice was given in 1662 of Margaret Mintie of Towny, now excommunicated for adultery, that "she should not reside within their parishes".[3] Margaret Fraser, the daughter of an Inverness schoolmaster, fled to London in 1674 after being excommunicated for failing to disclose the father of her child. The presbytery traced her there, and for at least two years sent messages to her, on one occasion by the Inverness merchants who visited London.[4]

A long process of penance awaited those who submitted to the presbytery. A good example is the case of James Gordoune and Janet Innes, referred to the Exercise of Alford by the Session of Kildrummie as guilty of adultery and "fugitive together". On 26 March 1663 they were publicly summoned and apparently began their penance. By 11 June they were living together again, and formal process was started against them. On 2 July Janet was doing penance at Towy, and by 23 July both were there. On 13 August they were reported to have finished their sentence at Towy and were sent to Kildrummie to do the same. On 3 September, 24 September and 8 October it was reported that they were still doing penance at Kildrummie. By 2 December James Gordoune had finished his sentence and was ready to be absolved, but Janet Innes had abandoned her penance. Process was ordered against her. James was absolved on 6 December, while the second summons was issued against Janet on 20 December and the third on 3 January. By 3 February Janet had appeared before the session again to accept her sentence. By 30 March she had satisfied at

---

[1] *Inverness and Dingwall*, p. 119.
[2] Ibid., p. xxxii.
[3] *Alford*, p. 8.   [4] *Inverness and Dingwall*, pp. 46–7, xxxi.

Kildrummie and Cabbrach and was ordered to Auchindoor. By 4 May she had satisfied all parishes and on 8 May was absolved.[1]

Apart from violations of the seventh commandment, cases of drunkenness, swearing, quarrels, violation of Sabbath discipline, slander, adherence to popery or quakerism, refusal to attend the parish church, charming and witchcraft came before the presbyteries.

Those who tried to resist the sentence of presbytery were faced by a long process which eventually would lead to excommunication. In 1668 the Synod of Aberdeen regularized this process for its area, although it was much the same in all of Scotland. The recalcitrant offender was to be thrice summoned by session, thrice summoned by presbytery, thrice publicly admonished, and thrice publicly prayed for. If the offender still refused to submit, he was recommended to the bishop for excommunication.[2] It is not surprising that most should submit to the presbytery before this process was over.

Excommunication was the most serious sentence imposed by the Church. There were two forms: lesser excommunication, which was suspension from Church privileges, and greater excommunication. The latter sentence was indeed a terrible one. Such a person was forbidden to leave the parish, to enter the house of any other person, or to have any contact with other parishioners.[3] Lesser excommunication could be imposed by a presbytery; greater excommunication required episcopal approval. The Synod of Aberdeen (1668) authorized three forms of excommunication: one to be pronounced against papists, one against Quakers, and one against those guilty of "grosse offences".[4]

The presbytery records of the period are filled with many cases of accusations, trials, and sentences. Many of the matters which

---

[1] *Alford*, pp. 12, 15–17, 20, 23–5, 35, 36, 40–42. Another illustration of the length of sentences was the order of the Synod of Aberdeen (1681) that ". . . single adulterers appear in publick for the space of halfe a year professing repentance, befor they be absolved, and that relapsers in adulterie do appeare for the space of a whole year, [and under no circumstances to] be absolved under a quarter of a year's publick appearances at least". *Alford*, p. 326.

[2] *Ibid.*, pp. 124–5.

[3] *Ibid.*, p. 402; *Dunkeld*, II, 52–3.

[4] *Alford*, pp. 126–8.

they handled would be dealt with by the police today. Nor can we assume that the large number of cases implies an especially immoral society—any more than a police blotter might imply the same about the twentieth century.[1]

The greatest weakness of presbyterian discipline was its tendency to become completely legalistic, thereby failing to arouse that true repentance which alone is worthy of the name. In some cases the discipline dramatically failed. Thus there was the case of the woman who so feared the humiliation of censure that she murdered her illegitimate child to avoid the "ignominy of the church pillory".[2] In other cases, a charitable solution was found only when the bishop intervened and overrode the recommendations of the church courts. The Synod of Aberdeen (1664) dealt with the case of five or six gentlemen of Strathdoune who "on the Lord's day, in the afternoon, at ane ailhouse, hade fallen into a strugle, and hade violently pursued one another with drawen swords, and the effusione of their bloods". The matter was a serious one because there were others "whose humors sufficiently prompt them to break out into the lyk wickedness". The synod recommended that they be referred to the High Commissioner for punishment. Instead the Bishop of Aberdeen met with them and the presbytery, at which time it was decided not to try to determine "who were mor who lesse guiltie, nor to inflict any censure". The offenders confessed their guilt, and were bound by the bishop "with a bond for their future peaceable and Christian behaviour".[3]

[1] Kirkton's thesis that these disciplinary cases represent a complete degeneration of church life, which before episcopacy was idyllic in its perfection, has been refuted many times. Kirkton wrote: "I have lived many years in a parish where I never heard an oath, and you might have ridden many miles before you had heard any: also, you could not for a great part of the country have lodged in a family where the Lord was not worshipped by reading, singing, and public prayer. Nobody complained more of our church government than our taverners, whose ordinary lamentation was, their trade was broken, people were become so sober." Pre-Restoration records of kirk-sessions and presbyteries testify to a good deal that Kirkton did not know about. The disciplinary cases of the Restoration are only too continuous with the kind of cases met in the era of the covenants. See Kirkton, *History*, pp. 48, 49, 64, 65; Grub, *History*, III, 161; *Alford*, pp. xxi–xxii. Also see below, p. 87, n. 4.
[2] *Domestic Annals*, II, 414.
[3] *Alford*, p. 45, 65.

Leighton also recognized the dangers of purely legal discipline and recommended to the clergy of Dunblane

> . . . frequent speaking with . . . [sinners] in private to the convinceing and awaking their consciences to a lively sinse of sin, and directing them in the exercises of repentance, and exhorting them to sett apart some tyme for a more solemne humbling of their soules in fasting and prayer, and not to admit them to publick confessioun untill they have, to our best discerneing, some real heart-sense of sine and remorse for it, and serious purposes of newness of life.[1]

In spite of their limitations, the presbyteries performed an essential function in the life of the Church of Scotland. Their frequent meetings brought the clergy of an area into close contact with one another—and that at a time when travel was not easy. The wide variety of their activities, and the considerable degree of authority which they could exercise, meant that they were the most important single element in the ordinary administration and discipline of the Restoration Church. Although there were limits to their authority, and their acts were subject to review by the synod, the large majority of cases were handled by the presbytery without reference to any other authority. The bishops were sometimes addressed as the Right Reverend Father in God, but to many who were summoned to appear before presbytery, that body must have seemed the real guardian of the Church.

SYNODS

Diocesan synods normally met twice a year, favourite months being April and October.[2] Sessions usually lasted for two or three days. All the members of the presbyteries within the bounds of the diocese were expected to attend, i.e. all of the ministers and expectants within the diocese. Requirements for attendance were similar in character to those used by presbyteries—absences were noted, excuses were accepted or rejected, and fines or other censures were imposed. The bishop presided at the synod, and the

---

[1] *Works*, II, 441.
[2] This was the practice of the Synod of Aberdeen, *Selections from Ecclesiastical Records of Aberdeen.*

synod did not meet if he could not be present. It is true that in
October 1663 Leighton's Synod of Dunblane met when he was
absent and that the "present Dean of Dunblane . . . in the
absence of the Bishope, did moderate".[1] This was most unusual,
the more normal custom being followed by Leighton three years
later when there was "no meeting of Synod in April 1666 as the
Bishop was in London".[2] The normal practice is only too clearly
seen in Leighton's letter to Lauderdale of 20 June 1674:

> . . . I receiv'd lately a letter from ye Dean of the Isles, complaining
> of ye great & many disorders in ye diocese for want of a Bishop. . . .
> He desir'd . . . that in ye interim for redresse of these disorders I
> would give warrant to them to meet in a diocesan synod & to appoint
> one to moderate in it, wch it seems hee thought I might doe, but I
> think not so, unles I have a particular comand for it.[3]

Synods had more of the character of a legislative body than of
a disciplinary court. Occasionally they did deal with specific disciplinary problems, but primarily they framed acts and resolu-
tions concerning the general discipline and worship of the Church.
The few changes in the worship of the Church made at the Restoration were embodied in acts of synod.[4] Since there were no
official canons, these acts of synod had something of the character
of canon law within each diocese.[5]

Synods were responsible for a variety of public duties. Thus the
Synod of Aberdeen (1688) decreed a day of "fasting, humiliation,
and prayer for a blessing on the seed season".[6] A census of the
papists of the kingdom was conducted by the various synods. One
of their most valuable activities was the support of numerous
public projects. Many of the roads, bridges, and harbour facilities
were built by contributions raised through the churches. The
Synod of Aberdeen ordered a collection to repair the "broken
bulwards of the town of Peterhead" (1662), and four years later a

---

[1] Butler, *Life and Letters of Leighton*, p. 369.   [2] Ibid., p. 375.
[3] *Lauderdale Papers*, III, 56.   [4] See below, p. 125 f.
[5] Although no official canons were ever approved, the introduction of a
Book of Canons (as well as a Liturgy) was considered by the bishops. *Lauderdale Papers*, II, Appendix, xxxiii. The pertinent section is quoted below, p. 132.
[6] *Banff*, II, 58.

general collection for the harbours of Kelburne and Innerkeithen was ordered.[1] Many of these projects were first recommended by Act of Parliament or the Privy Council, and the synod passed such requests on to the ministers of the diocese.

Another important duty was the supervision of the books of each presbytery and the privy censure of the presbyteries. Examiners were appointed to inspect the books. In 1664 the Synod of Aberdeen ordered that presbytery books were to be sent in to the bishop twenty days before meetings of synod in order that the records might be examined with "quick dispatch".[2] During the privy censure of synod, each presbytery would in turn be removed, and the remaining brethren examine its activities.

The synod, like the other Church courts, worked closely with the civil magistrate. This co-operation was dramatically demonstrated at the first meeting of the Synod of Edinburgh (October 1662) when

> to countenance this meeting, which consisted of 58 ministeris, the Kingis advocat, and my Lord Tarbet ane of the lordis of his Majesteis Counsell and Session, with the Provest and bailleis of Edinburgh, wer present.[3]

Nor was this alignment purely formal. In 1671 the Synod of Moray received the case of Mr John Mackintosh, who was a brother of the laird of Aberarder and had been publicly rebuked by his minister in Deviot. Whereupon John waited for the minister at the church door and said: "You base raskall, how durst yee bee so peart as to abuse mee yis day? yee was too bold to doe it, yee might have used your own equalls so and not me . . . were not for little to mee I wold bruiss yor bones." Within two months he submitted and announced that "he would yield obedience to Church discipline". The reason for this sudden change of heart was made clear a few weeks later when it was reported that "Jon Mcintosh . . . is constantlie from home searching for money to pay the Earle of Morray the fyne that was imposed judiciallie on him for his former opprobrious speeches to his Minister".[4] On

---

[1] *Alford*, pp. 4, 79.   [2] Ibid., p. 56.
[3] *Nicoll*, p. 381.   [4] *Inverness and Dingwall*, pp. 14–17.

11 October 1682 the Synod of Aberdeen noted several parliamentary laws against Sabbath breaking and recommended to the brethren that they "be strict in executing the censures of the church against such offenders, and that they seek the concurrence of the Civill power to restraine them as the laws of the land do allow".[1]

The most difficult question to determine was the relation between the bishop and the other members of the synod. Row declared that at such a synod the "bishop . . . did all by sole jurisdiction [and none of the ministers] had the freedom of a vote, but all come there to be censured".[2] Row's strong dislike of the Restoration Church may well have coloured his understanding of the proceedings of the synod. The Synod of Dunblane certainly followed a different procedure under Leighton :

> It was declared [in 1663] by the Bischope that the Synod and each member of it hath now as full and free libertie of voting and declaring their assent and dissent in all things that occur as ever they had in the former tymes.[3]

Leighton's practice was often more generous than that of most bishops. Yet almost universally synodical decisions were enacted by "the Bishope, with consent of the brethren of the Synod",[4] so that the decisions were not just the arbitrary ones of a bishop imposed on the synod. At the same time, the bishop's position was hardly analogous with that of a moderator in a presbytery. The bishop had a negative veto over any action of the synod, and his general authority over the discipline of the clergy, as well as his important civil status, probably gave considerable weight to his recommendations. There is no evidence of any serious conflict between the bishop and his synod, and probably those who conformed to the settlement were willing to follow his lead in synodical matters.

THE NATIONAL SYNOD

In the early years of the Restoration a National Synod was favoured by Charles.[5] Lauderdale also wrote (1661) to Sharp that

---

[1] *Alford*, p. 335.   [2] Row, *Life of Blair*; quoted in *Dunkeld*, I, 60.
[3] Butler, *Life and Letters of Leighton*, p. 369.
[4] *Alford*, p. 6.   [5] Printed in Stephen, *Life of Sharp*, p. 284.

"I . . . shall expect to heare from you concerning ane Assembly when you there finde it seasonable".[1] In 1663 an Act of Parliament authorized a National Synod to be composed of the archbishops and bishops, the deans and archdeacons, the moderator and a minister from each presbytery, and representatives from the universities. The Archbishop of St Andrews was to preside. They could meet only with royal approval and consider such matters as were submitted to them in the name of the King; no Act passed by them would be valid unless approved by the Archbishop of St Andrews and the King. This National Synod never met, and the concerted effort by a group of reforming bishops and presbyters to call it in 1674 was a complete failure.[2] The tensions of the time were too great; Lauderdale feared that such a synod would question his political position, and the memory of the fateful synod of 1638 had not been forgotten. "A burn'd Child dreads the fire", he wrote.[3]

The basic structure of the judicatories of the Church of Scotland was not altered in any important or significant way at the Restoration. The courts continued to meet much as they had before, and to do the same things. The Calvinist ideal of order and discipline still governed their activities,[4] and the courts remained important administrative units as well.

The new factor was the relation of this whole structure to the episcopate. There was a very real integration of authority on an administrative level. Although courts continued to function much as before, at every crucial point episcopal authority was also essential. The curious fact is, that within the terms of the settlement, bishops were important, and even essential, in the efficient administration of the Church. At the same time the restoration of episcopacy failed to alter in any significant way that ideal of the

---

[1] *Miscellany of the Scottish History Society*, I, 249.
[2] See above, p. 24.
[3] *Lauderdale Papers*, III, 53.
[4] However, this ideal was not prosecuted with quite as much success. There was undoubtedly some lowering of general morality after the accession of Charles II. The Restoration Parliament in Scotland has been given the title, "The Drunken Parliament".

Christian life which the pre-Restoration courts had also sought
to foster.[1]

[1] A visiting Englishman recognized this unusual situation. He wrote: "However, tho' their Kirk-Sessions and Presbyteries savour of the Presbyterian
Classes, and are, as one might conceive, derived from 'em, and follow 'em close
in the Methods of Governing the People, yet because they allow and respect
the Name of Bishop, and give him an Account at their Six Months Synods of
what they did in their Presbyteries and Parishes, because as Perpetual Moderator he influenced their Consultations, and had the Power of Mission and
Ordination as with us; therefore this Government of their Church was called
Episcopal, tho' hardly to be discern'd for such, by Travellers who have seen
what Episcopacy is in other places." Morer, *Short Account*, p. 49.

5

THE PARISH CLERGY OF THE KIRK

THE Restoration Church of Scotland can never be accused
of having had an uneducated clergy. Strict requirements for
training were maintained, being dispensed only in the most
unusual circumstances. Each student was expected to complete
his education at one of the four great universities (Aberdeen,
St Andrews, Edinburgh, Glasgow) and then to spend some years,
usually four, in the study of divinity before taking his trials or
examination. In 1664 the Synod of Aberdeen ordered "none to be
tried until they have studied divinity some years after they be
graduatt unless extraordinar pregnancie in learning be seen in
them", and in 1673 this was made more specific. Noting that
many had entered their trials before a sufficient study of divinity
had been completed, whereby "many are entered who are not
fitted nor qualified for that office . . . it is appoynted that, befor
any . . . enter upon tryalls . . . they have been full four yeirs
graduate befor, and have imployed their tyme in the Studie of
Divinitie".[1]

A student's life in the universities could be an arduous one. In
1672 an English Nonconformist who came north to study at the
University of Glasgow wrote of his life there.

> I was admitted in the Batchelor year, having studied Logic and
> Philosophy so long in England, and came under the presidency and
> tuition of that celebrated philosopher Mr John Tran. . . . I soon
> found my great account in it, to sit constantly at his feet, for as keen
> as my appetite was to learning, here was rich provision enough to
> satisfy it, in daily dictates, disputations, etc.
> The good orders of the College were very agreeable to mine
> inclination. At five o'clock in the morning the bell rings, and every

[1] *Alford*, pp. 58, 200.

scholar is to answer to his name, which is then called over. The day is spent in private studies and public exercises in the classes; at nine at night every chamber is visited by the respective regents. The Lord's days strictly observed, all the scholars called to the several classes, where, after religious exercises, all attend the Primar and Regents to church, forenoon and afternoon, and in the same order from church. Then, in the evening, called again to the classes, and then come under examination concerning the sermons heard, and give account of what was appointed the foregoing Sabbath in some theological treatise . . . and then to supper and chambers.[1]

When Marischal College was founded in Aberdeen in 1593, the foundation charter specified a curriculum which showed considerable continuity with earlier ideals of education. The Principal must "be well versed in the Scriptures, able to unfold the mysteries of faith", and skilled in languages, "especially in Hebrew and in Syriac, which we wish to be spread abroad". Students also studied the "Physiology from the Greek text of Aristotle"; a short explanation of anatomy, geography, and history; the outlines of astronomy, and Hebrew grammar; the elements of arithmetic and geometry; and "selections from Aristotle's books of Ethics and Politics from the Greek text, to which he shall add Cicero's books *De Officiis* [in order to] extend acquaintance with the Latin tongue".[2]

In 1669 Gilbert Burnet became Professor of Divinity at the University of Glasgow. His account of the training which his students of divinity received makes clear that their preparation was a serious matter:

On Monday I made all the students in course explain a part of the body of Divinity in Latin with a thesis, and answer all the arguments. On Tuesday I had a prelection in Latin, in which I designed to go through a body of Divinity in ten or twelve years. . . . On Wednesday I went through a critical commentary on St Matthew's gospel which I delivered in English. . . . On Thursday I expounded a Psalm in Hebrew, comparing it with the 70, the vulgar and our version. And by turns on Thursday I explained the Constitution and the ritual, and made the Apostolical canons my text, bringing every

[1] *Source Book of Scottish History*, III, 421–2.
[2] *Records of Marischal College and University*, I, 63.

particular I opened to them to one of the canons. On Friday I made the students in course preach a short sermon upon a text that I gave them and . . . shewed them what was defective or amiss in the sermon, and how the text ought to have been opened and applied. Besides all this, I called them all together in the evening every day to prayers. I read a parcel of Scripture, and after I had explained it I made a short sermon for a quarter of an hour upon it. I then asked them what difficulties they met with in their studies and answered such questions as they put to me. Thus I applied myself for eight months in the year.[1]

There is some indication that the universities themselves had suffered during the late troubles and were in need of further financial resources. Parliament passed several Acts to relieve the "mean and incompetent provision of the Masters and professors thairof [which] is so prejudiciall to the floorishing of these seminaries of Church and State, that vnles some considerable augmentation be setled vpon them for their encouragement the ablest and fittest persons . . . will shun and avoid the vndertaking of functions in Vniversities".[2] In 1664 Parliament ordered all vacant stipends (i.e. income from parishes which had no minister) to be given to the universities for seven years, and in 1672 this legislation was renewed for another seven-year period. In 1663 a tax was placed on all bishops of "fiftie punds for every thousand merks" of income, which was to be paid to the universities. This tax was to last for five years.[3] Even so, as late as 1686 complaints were still made about the quality of the universities. The Earl of Perth wrote to the Archbishop of Canterbury that "so soon as we can get the lenth of puting the Universities in order, (a work I have my heart much sett upon,) I hope a few years will give us a better clergie, for at present wee are undone by the want of such . . .".[4] Nevertheless, it is clear that the Church of Scotland expected her clergy to obtain the best education that was possible in Scotland at that time.

[1] Clarke and Foxcroft, *Life of Burnet*, p. 82.
[2] *Records of Marischal College and University*, i, 309.
[3] Ibid., pp. 309, 310, 313, 314. A lesser tax was to be paid by ministers.
[4] Clarke, *Collection of Letters*, p. 77. The letter is undated, but very probably was written shortly after the accession of James VII.

The financial burden upon students for such a long period of education was considerable, and aid was given to them in several ways. Often large gifts or "mortifications" would be left by generous donors, the interest from which would be used to support one or two students in a university. James Milne (1677), burgess of Aberdeen, left a mortification of 2500 marks to support two students in Marischal College. The money was to be held by the "Provest Bailyies and counsell of . . . Abd . . . And the annuallrent therof to be yearely employed . . . for mantain-ance . . . of tuo schollars".[1] Although such support would not invariably be given to a student who planned to study divinity, undoubtedly many students did receive help from the numerous mortifications of the period.

The pre-Restoration practice of having a seminarian (or "bursar") supported by each presbytery was also continued during the Restoration. The Synod of St Andrews (1662) "recom-mended to the several Presbyteries that they be careful to have the bursaries, which they maintain in the New College, filled with hopeful, able and pious young men: and that they take care of the timeous payment of the proportions laid upon the parishes".[2] In 1675 it was further required that the "bursar"

> continue at his studies during the space of five months at least; and that at his return he bring with him a testimonial to the Presbytery . . . of his Virtuous carriage, obedience to the Masters, diligence in his Studies, and the evidence and fruit of his academical exercises".[3]

The Synod of Aberdeen (1685) required "bursars" to be in residence from 1 December to 1 June, and ordered their stipend to be reduced if they arrived late or left early.[4] The previous year the synod had dealt with a case of "bursars" who "afterwards turned of to secular imployments" and recommended that the "bursars" be carefully chosen hereafter and "oblidge themselves to follow their studies in order to the ministerie".[5]

The method of appointment varied somewhat, and might be by the presbytery, by the bishop, alternately by the presbytery and

---

[1] *Marischal College*, I, 317–19.   [2] *Dunkeld*, II, 120.
[3] Ibid.   [4] *Alford*, p. 367.   [5] Ibid., p. 360.

bishop, or by recommendation of the presbytery, subject to approval by the bishop. A case of the latter was Mr John Fyff, who was appointed "the bursar of Presbytery [of Dunkeld] on condition that the approval of the Bishop of Dunkeld be obtained".[1] The appointment was ordinarily for four years.

The money for the "bursar" was raised by an assessment upon each minister. The Synod of Aberdeen (1669) ordered "bursars'" fees to be paid, "to witt, twentie shilling for ilk hundreth communicants",[2] and the Presbytery of Dingwall required "50 shil. each man for the divinitie burser agt the nixt day". The pattern of the next meeting was only too typical, however. At this meeting, "the Bretheren for the most part declynes to pay the burse to Mr John Mckenzie this yeir, pretending they payed him at once for both this yeir and the last".[3]

Occasionally, men were sent to England to study. In 1637 four scholarships had been founded by John Warner, Bishop of Rochester, to support students from Scotland at Balliol College. The Archbishop of Canterbury was patron, and students from Scotland continued to be presented after the Restoration.[4]

After a student had finished his academic study, he began his trials or examinations for licensing as an expectant or preacher. There were actually two forms or "orders" of the lower clergy—expectants, who were not ordained but simply licensed by the bishop; and ministers, who received ordination and collation from the bishop and were presented to a benefice. Separate trials were held for each "order"—a man ordinarily became first an expectant and later a minister.

Men were admitted to trials only on licence from the bishop. On 28 November 1676 the Presbytery of Dingwall recorded that "Maister Collin Douglesse (who obtained libertie from the Bishop to enter on tryalls at the preceeding Synod) delivered a comon head *de Lumine interno*".[5] The trials were thorough

---

[1] *Dunkeld*, I, 229. For examples of other methods of appointment, see *Dunkeld*, II, 118–24.
[2] *Alford*, p. 93.   [3] *Inverness and Dingwall*, p. 306.
[4] Clarke, *Collection of Letters*, p. 109.
[5] *Inverness and Dingwall*, p. 394. See also *Alford*, p. 7.

examinations conducted by the presbytery at its regular meetings. The examination was held over a period of six or more meetings, so that the whole process often took months. In 1671 the Synod of Aberdeen set forth standards for examination which were typical of the period. They ordered that

> evrie young man who passes his tryalls shall have six dyets for that effect, and 1. he shall sustaine the tryall of the Languages, 2. his questionarie tryall, 3. the Exegesis, 4. his dispute, 5. he shall have the Exercise and Additione, and 6. a popular sermon.

During these trials, presbytery was to be sure that the student was

> acquainted in competent measure with the letter and received sense of Scripture, positive and polemicall Divinitie, and Church Historie, [and that he] be so weell at least acquainted with the originall Languages, as to expone any chapter in the Greek New Testament, and read any parcell of the Old Testament in Hebrew.[1]

In the vast majority of cases the candidates were approved,[2] although certification was not automatic. On 22 November 1671 Mr Patrick Coplend was told that his popular sermon "was no fruits of his studies but was taken almost verbatim out of Sedgwick upon the 54 of Isaiah".[3] The Presbytery of Dingwall also found difficulty with the trials of one of its candidates:

> That day [16 May 1667] no exercise. Mr John Bain, Student in divinity, having ane exigesis de Notis Ecclesiae, and disputes theranent, which the Bretheren taking to ther consideratione, judged him to be somewhat confused in both, and advised him to acquaint himself better with the theological controversies that he might the better enable himself for the ministry.[4]

Once the candidate had satisfied the presbytery, he was recommended to the bishop for the "opening of his mouth",[5] or licensing as a preacher. Though the licence was ordinarily issued by the bishop, it was sometimes given by presbytery in the absence

---

[1] Alford, pp. 176–7.
[2] Inverness and Dingwall, p. 318; Alford, pp. 22–3.   [3] Alford, p. 180.
[4] Inverness and Dingwall, p. 319.   [5] Ibid., p. 7.

of the bishop. This right was specifically recognized in 1663 by the Synod of Aberdeen, which gave the moderator permission to license men to preach when the bishop was "absent out of his Kingdom".[1]

A visiting Englishman wrote that after the preacher "gets the Licence, he commences Probationer for the Ministry, and commonly continues such for two, three, four, or more Years therafter, till he is presented to some Benefice".[2]

An expectant or a student in divinity could receive presentation to a benefice. Presentation was always directed to the bishop, and upon his licence, the candidate began his ordination trials with presbytery. Even expectants who had undergone previous trials were required to pass the ordination examination. However, the examination was almost identical with that taken by an applicant for an expectant's licence. Upon satisfactory completion, the candidate was recommended to the bishop for collation and ordination.

As is the case with examiners in every age, it was sometimes difficult to know whether or not to approve a given candidate. The Presbytery of Alford recommended Mr James Irvine with some misgivings. His trials had been unsatisfactory on 19 September, 6 February, and again on 20 March 1677. Finally on 10 April he had another trial and language examination:

> He was as yet found ignorant in the Greek, and although he did not give such abundant satisfaction in his other tryall's, yet the pluralitie of the Presbytrie, from a compassionat consideration of the case of the people of Cabrach, and of the condition of the said Mr James who promised to improve himselfe, more and more by prayer and studie, did recomend him to the Lord Bishop for ordination.[3]

Since a man did not enter his trials for the ministry until he had already been presented to a benefice, the bishop frequently required the presbytery to accelerate the examinations so that the candidate could more quickly begin his work in the parish. On 20 October 1672 the Presbytery of Inverness learned by letter that "the Bishope desyred that the Presbyterie should accelerat the

---

[1] *Alford*, p. 33.   [2] Morer, *Short Account*, p. 44.   [3] *Alford*, p. 292.

tryells of Mr Michael ffraser".[1] The subsequent behaviour of Mr Fraser, who was eventually deprived for a short period, suggests that an accelerated programme was not always a wise one.

On very rare occasions, a man would be ordained by the bishop without trials. On 5 May 1685 the Presbytery of Meigle reported this unusual practice :

> This day Mr. Alexander Mackenzie, student in Divinitie, presented to the church of Newtyle, offered a letter to the Presbiterie directed from my Lord Bishop of Dunkeld, anent his admission to the church of Newtyle, he having already been put in orders of a presbiter, and received letters of collation from my Lord St Andrews his Grace.

The Presbytery thought it best to delay the matter for eight days, but dared delay it no longer. At that time

> . . . the letter from My Lord Bishop of Dunkeld . . . was publicely read . . . in obedience to which the Presbiterie appointed the minister of Blair to preach at Newtyle, and to admit the said Mr. Alexander Mackenzie to the free exercise of his ministry.[2]

Although technically legal, this violation of the customary procedure was not tried again by Bishop Bruce. Usually men received collation and ordination from the bishop after the presbytery signified its approval. Collation and ordination were performed only by the bishop. When he was absent or unavailable, another bishop was called upon for this purpose. Thus on 26 March 1663 the Presbytery of Alford reported that Mr Walter Ritchie had been instituted minister of Touch, "he having received letters of collatione from the Archbishop of St Andrews, being ordained by his vicar, the Bishop of Edinburgh, our Ordinarie not being yet established".[3] The practice of ordination by the bishop was quite universal according to all the extant records available, and none of the exceptions which were permissible in the licensing of preachers occurred when ordination was in question.

Those who sought ordination came to the bishop, and the service usually took place in his church. One of Gilbert Burnet's

---

[1] *Inverness and Dingwall*, p. 32; v. sup., pp. 44–5.   [2] *Dunkeld*, I, 228–9.
[3] *Alford*, p. 11.

"greviences and abuses" was the failure of the Scottish bishops to ordain men in their own parish churches:

> . . . if in yor Ordinations ye followed St Cyprians rule, yow would ordain plebe praesente et diligente, and go to the Churches where they are to serve and there marry ym to their people. This would be infinitly more grave and solemn than to transact it wt three or four Ministers in the church next yor residence.[1]

One bishop who did hold his ordinations in the parish church of the ordinand was Robert Leighton. On 15 November 1667 the Bishop of Dunblane and five presbyters went to the Kirk of Port to examine and ordain Mr James Donaldson to be the minister of that church.[2] On the same day, Mr Donaldson also received collation and institution from the bishop by the hands of the moderator and dean.

One of the concessions which Leighton offered in his Accommodation Scheme was that

> . . . Entrants being lawfully presented by the Patron, and duly tried by the Presbytery, there shall be a day agreed upon by the Bishop and Presbytery for their meeting together for their solemn Ordination and admission, at which there shall be one appointed to preach, and that it shall be at the Parish Church to which they are to be admitted, except in cases of impossibility or extreme inconvenience.[3]

The diaconate was almost non-existent in Scotland at this time, and the ordination mentioned is ordination as a minister or presbyter. There are, however, a few references to the diaconate as a distinct order of the ministry. In 1685 the Synod of St Andrews ordered that "noe prisbiter or deacone" should perform marriage ceremonies without proper proclamation of the banns.[4] Doctor Munro also referred to the Order: ". . . our Ecclesiastical Superiors, who ordained Priests and Deacons according to the forms of the Church of England".[5] Especially interesting is the

---

[1] *Miscellany of the Scottish History Society*, II, 352.
[2] Butler, *Life and Letters of Leighton*, p. 581.
[3] Ibid., p. 444; quoted from MS.
[4] *Dunkeld*, II, 86.   [5] *Presbyterian Inquisition*, p. 30.

record of the ordination of a deacon by the Bishop of Orkney in 1683:

> [The oaths being tendered] with all other ceremonie usual in such cases, [the Bishop] gave him full power to administer the Sacrament of Baptisme, and to give the benefits of mariage, to visit the sick, keep sessions, or any other offices that are incumbent for a deacone to perform, restricting him only from the actual consecratione of the Lord's Supper.[1]

But references to the diaconate in the traditional sense are very rare. At most, they indicate that deacons were not unheard of in the Restoration Church, and perhaps that the reforming movement revived the diaconate in a few places.[2]

Considerable uncertainty exists about the form of ordination used, and it doubtless varied. There is some testimony as to the influence of the English ordinal on Scottish practice. Wodrow writes:

> To give every man his due, he [Alexander Burnet of Glasgow] was certainly one of the best morals among the present clergy. . . . He was a mighty bigot for the English ceremonies and forms, and as forward to have all the usages of that church introduced to Scotland, as if he had been educated by bishop Laud; yea, to have his fancy pleased with these pagentries, he could have almost submitted to the old claim of the see of York over the church of Scotland. At his first diocesan meeting, he put five or six of his curates publicly in orders after the English pontifical to inure the west of Scotland to these novelties.[3]

William Row, in his reference to the ordination of James Weems in 1663, may also be referring to the English ordinal. He

---

[1] Craven, *History of the Church in Orkney*, p. 102; quoted in *Scottish Historical Review*, October 1954, p. 173.

[2] Their existence was not known to Gilbert Burnet. In his "Memorial of Grievances" he wrote: "Our want of Deacons is as essential as any relating to Government can be: for I am assured more can be said for proving ym to be *jure divino* than Bishops . . .", *Miscellany of the Scottish History Society*, II, 352. The Scottish Ordinal of 1620 has no form of ordination for a deacon. It contains only "The form and manner of ordaining ministers, and of consecrating archbishops and bishops, used in the Church of Scotland", *Miscellany of the Wodrow Society*, p. 591.

[3] *History*, II, 8.

wrote that "the Bishop did read all of the prayers and questions etc. out of the Service Book and Book of Ordination".[1] However, there is less indication of English influence on ordinations than on the consecration of bishops.[2]

There was, of course, no official or authorized ordinal,[3] and the Scottish Church seems to have developed its own rite for the ordination of a presbyter as it had done for the consecration of a bishop. This was apparently the case in an ordination by Bishop Honeyman of Orkney in 1666. After the oaths of allegiance, supremacy and canonical obedience were administered,

> . . . the deuties of the ministrie were held forth to him fully, and hee exhorted to the conscionable performance thereof by the said Andrew, Lord Bischope of Orkney; and thereafter, by prayer and impositione of hands, the said Mr John was admitted to the work of the ministrie in the church of Evie and Randall in Orkney. My Lord Bischope closed the actione with prayer.[4]

The development of a Scottish rite is clear in the account of an ordination by Bishop Mackenzie in 1678. "My Lord Bischope and the Brethren went on to his ordanatione according to the order of the Church of Scotland."[5]

Extant descriptions of ordinations invariably refer to the imposition of hands. Thus Bishop Mackenzie ". . . did admitte him to the forsaid kirkes by the impositione of hands".[6] In an ordination by Robert Leighton in 1667, it was recorded that "the said reverend Bishop did thairafter by caling upon God most high and impositione of hands with the presbyterie ordean and admitt the said Mr James Donaldson minister of the Gospell of Jesus Christ, afterwards giving him the Holy Bible and wyth hand of fellowship of both Bishop and presbiterie".[7]

[1] *Life of Blair*, p. 443, quoted in *Scottish Historical Review*, October 1954, p. 169.
[2] Donaldson, "Scottish Ordinations in the Restoration Period", *Scottish Historical Review*, October 1954.
[3] The Scottish ordinal of 1620 may have been regarded by some as an authorized ordinal. However, it was not universally used. See also above, p. 39 f.
[4] *Scottish Historical Review*, October, 54, p. 172.
[5] Ibid.   [6] Ibid.   [7] Butler, *Life and Letters of Leighton*, p. 581.

The Gordon case [1] suggests that the Scottish ordinal of 1620 [2] may still have influenced ordinations in the Restoration. In Gordon's petition to Clement XI, he claimed that the "heretics . . . have cast away the Catholic form and changed it into this: Take thou authority to preach the Word of God and to minister His holy Sacraments".[3] Gordon's reference may have been to the English ordinal, but it is also quite possible that the form quoted came from the Scottish ordinal of 1620. In the English rite, the sentence "Take thou authority . . ." is not said at the imposition of hands, but at the delivery of the Bible, while in the Scottish ordinal it is part of the actual sentence of ordination.[4]

After the minister had been ordained, he would receive collation from the bishop, who would then issue instructions to the presbytery to institute him into his parish church. According to Wodrow, "one of the ordinary clauses of collations was, 'I do hereby receive him into the function of the holy ministry'".[5] The Act of Parliament (1662) requiring presentation from a patron and collation from the bishop was especially unacceptable to nonconforming clergy, and was the immediate cause of their withdrawal from the Establishment in 1662–3.

The bishop usually did not attend the institution, but issued a letter to presbytery authorizing them to admit the new minister to his parish. A typical letter was that from Andrew Bruce, Bishop of Dunkeld, to the Presbytery of Meigle in 1686:

REVEREND BRETHREN,
These ar to desyr you, ife there be no objection made by the heritors and parishonars of Alyght against Mr John Lowsan his admission to the ministrie in the said parish, that you may proceid to give him admission and institution thereto, and, for that end, appoynt on[e] to preach on the day wheron yee resolve so to doe.

[1] See above, p. 41 f.
[2] Printed in *Miscellany of the Wodrow Society*, pp. 591 ff.
[3] Lowndes, *Vindication*, II, cxix.
[4] The ordination prayer of the 1620 ordinal is: "In the name of God, and by the authoritie committed unto us by the Lord Jesus Christ, wee give unto thee power and authoritie to preach the Word of God, to minister his holie Sacraments, and exercise Discipline." *Miscellany of the Wodrow Society*, 605.
[5] *History*, I, 265.

This, with my p[r]ayers for the blessing of Almighty God to mak your
labors in the work of the Gospell successfull, is all at present from,
Your very loving brothr in the Lord,
A. DUNKELDEN

Such men were not forced on a parish, and the parishioners had
a formal right to approve the appointment of their minister. Thus
a meeting was held of the "heritors, members of Session, indwellers
and parishonars of the towne and parish of Alyght . . . to propone
and give in their objections why Mr John Lowsan . . . should
not be admitted. . . . Non compeird in his contrar." Only after
the parish had signified its assent did the presbytery make plans
for the formal institution.[1]

The formal admission and institution was an important public
service. It usually took place on a Sunday, and delegates from the
presbytery presided and instituted the new minister. In 1676 the
Presbytery of Inverness received a report from

> Mr Thomas Huison and Mr James Grant . . . that according to
> the Bishops order they were at Kilchuimen upon the 12 of March,
> being the Lords day, and Mr Thomas Huison did preach . . . and
> after sermone delivered to the said Mr Robert Monroe the sacred
> bible, and the keys of the Churches doors, with the books of dis-
> cipline, as is usuall in such cases, seriously exhorting him to humility,
> fidelity, and sedulity in his future ministeriall function, and im-
> mediatly therafter all the gentlemen and elders put did cordially
> and unanimously, by reaching furth of their hands, signifying and
> declaring by this their acceptance of the said Mr Robert Monroe for
> their future Minister in these respective bounds of Abertarfe and
> Glenmoriston, promiseing obedience, faithfulness, and assistance to
> him, according to their severall power and charge.
>
> [Also] . . . the said Mr Thomas declared that he gave the said
> Mr Robert reall possession and infeftment in the manse and gleib by
> delivering to him timber, stone, and earth, as is usuall in such cases.[2]

With minor variations [3] this seems to have been the usual form
for institution.

---

[1] *Dunkeld*, I, 230–31. Another example was the admission of Mr Alexander
Cuming to the parish of Moy and Dallarassie. *Inverness and Dingwall*, p. 96.
[2] *Inverness and Dingwall*, pp. 68–9.
[3] See, for example, *Dunkeld*, I, 56; *Inverness and Dingwall*, p. 36.

There is some question about the status of men who had received presbyterian ordination and who conformed in 1662. As there had been no episcopal ordinations in Scotland for more than twenty years, a large number of the conforming clergy must have been in this category. Much of the material on this subject has recently been summarized by the Reverend Steward Mechie in an article entitled "Episcopacy in Post-Reformation Scotland".[1] Reordination of men with presbyterian ordination does seem to have been considered and in a few cases practised. In 1662 Alexander Brodie wrote that "I spok with Mr Wm. Falconer to adviz the Bishop to moderation, and to lay noe bands on Ministers . . .".[2] At no later time does Brodie complain about his advice being ignored. In 1690 a letter written from Scotland (by Mr John Sage?) describes the persecution of the "Episcopalians" by the "Presbyterians". Among those preaching "against the Pride of Prelates" was Doctor Robinson, one of the Ministers of Edinburgh. The letter goes on to describe the "Doctor, whose great complaint it has been of late, that he has groan'd these twenty seven Years by-past under the Yoke of Episcopacy, although at the Restitution of the Government, he did not think his Mission good, having had only Presbyterial Ordination; and therefore was re-ordained by a Bishop".[3] Mr Mechie also believes that both Skinner and Grub may have recorded authentic traditions about reordination. Bishop Skinner writes:

> Others who had entered with orders only from the Presbyteries, or as some did, at their own hands, without any formal ordination at all, either were ordained anew by the Bishops, which mightily offended the outstanders; or where circumstances appeared favourable, were received on their submission and swearing canonical obedience to the Bishop, and by him enpowered to exercise the office and function of Presbyters in the church, according to the present constitution.[4]

---

[1] *Scottish Journal of Theology*, 1955, pp. 20 ff.
[2] *Diaries of the Lairds of Brodie*, p. 274.
[3] *An Account of the Persecution of the Church in Scotland*, pp. 41–2.
[4] Skinner, *An Ecclesiastical History of Scotland*, p. 462. Also Mechie, pp. 32–3.

Grub writes: "Ordination was conferred by the bishops, with the assistance of their presbyters: but none of them, except Bishop Mitchell [Bishop of Aberdeen, 1662–3], insisted on reordaining ministers who had received only Presbyterian ordination, though they did not refuse to do so when asked." [1]

Yet such reordination was certainly very rare. Wodrow is hardly reticent in listing grievances against the bishops, but he exonerates them from this charge. "Our Scots bishops, by submitting to be reordained as presbyters, [the reordination of Leighton and Sharp in London] declared to all the world that they did not believe their presbyterian ordination to be valid; and yet when they came down to Scotland, and entered upon the exercise of their episcopal office, they did not reordain such of the ministers as complied with them." [2] Robert Leighton, in a letter on the Accommodation, makes the same point:

> . . . though no ordinations may pass without a Bishop, that is only in regard to the exercise of that power, but doth not stop the presbyters simply of the power, or say, their ordination without a Bishop is null: since the Bishops in Scotland do not attempt the reordination of those whom presbytery had ordained. [3]

Mr Mechie's conclusion is certainly warranted. " . . . While reordination almost certainly took place in some areas and possibly in others, too, when it was requested, it was not universal and not even general." [4]

The duties which were expected of a parish minister were clearly set forth in the visitation records of the time. The questions contained in the "Directions for the visitation of Churches" issued by the Synod of Aberdeen in 1675 indicate the duties expected of a Restoration minister. The elders, heritors, and masters of families were asked

1. If there be preaching on the Lord's day and how often;
2. If the minister preaches to their edification, and be carefull in reproveing sinne, both privatlie and publicklie . . .

---

[1] Grub, *History*, III, 218; also Mechie, p. 33.   [2] *History*, I, 239.
[3] Butler, *Life and Letters of Leighton*, p. 428.   [4] Mechie, op. cit., p. 34.

H

3. If he keep at home, not stirring abroad unnecessarilie;
4. If his conversatione be without lightnes or vanitie, grave and exemplarie in pietie;
5. If he doe, without necessitie resort to taverns;
6. If he administrat the sacrament of the Lord's Supper, and how often in the yeir;
7. If he be carefull to debarr from it all such as are scandalous;
8. If discipline be diligentlie and impartiallie exercised;
9. If he be carefull to visit the sick when he is informed, and called therto;
10. If he be a good example to the people in ordering his owne familie;
11. If he visite the townes and families in his parochine, and excite them to pietie . . .
12. If he be diligent in catechiseing, especiallie in taking paines to prepare young persones befor they partake of the Lord's Supper;
13. If he be carefull to maintaine and promote peace and love among all people . . .[1]

Ministers were regularly expected to preach twice on Sunday, catechize weekly, celebrate the Lord's Supper once a year, visit the sick, make parish calls, administer discipline, and take care of the poor. Where there was a school, this was also supervised by the minister. The Presbytery of Fordyce, in 1674, recorded their report on Master Alexander Seton, minister of Banff since 1661. They found "discipline weell observed, catechiseing twyse in the year and communione celebrat, with great pains taken by the minister in preaching on the Sabbath and lectureing on the Tuesday, care of the school, poor, and mortifications, and texts of scripture and preachers punctualie sett doune, wherwith the Presbytery was weell satisfied". [2]

Ministers were expected to reside in their parishes. There is nothing comparable to the system of absentee incumbents and curates which was found in England at this time. The Synod of Dunblane ordered that no minister be absent from his parish for more than two consecutive weeks without episcopal permission.[3] Nor was this limited to Dunblane. In 1675 Mr Gilbert Marshall

---

[1] *Alford*, p. 232.   [2] *Banff*, II, 42.   [3] *Dunkeld*, I, 57.

reported to the Presbytery of Inverness that "he prached at Dunlichity on Dec. 27, according to the Lord Bishope and Sub-synods order, and rebuked the Minr, Mr Michael Fraser, for his long absence from his charge".[1]

Robert Leighton set forth the highest ideals for the clergy of his diocese. In an address to the Synod of Dunblane in 1667, he proposed the following questions:

1. Whether he be constantly assiduous in plain and profitable preaching, . . . fitting his doctrine to the capacities . . . of all sorts within his charge?

2. Whether he be diligent in catechising . . . throughout the year, . . . and not wholly casting it over upon some few days or weeks near the time of communion?

3. How often in the year he celebrates the holy communion? for I am ashamed to say, whether, at least, once every year?

4. Whether he does faithfully and impartially exercise discipline. . . .

5. Whether he be diligent . . . to know the deportment of the several families and persons of his flock; and do frequently visit the families, and . . . do his best certainly to inform himself, whether they constantly use morning and evening prayer, together with reading of the Scriptures. . . .

6. Whether he be careful of the relief of the poor, and of visiting the sick, whensoever he knows of any, even though they neglect to send for him.

7. Whether he does in private . . . admonish those he knows . . . to be given to uncleanness. . . .

8. Whether he watches exactly over his own conversation.

9. Whether he spend the greatest portions of his time in private, in reading, and prayer, and meditation.

10. Whether he makes it the great business, and withal the great pleasure, of his life, to fulfil the work of his ministry, in the several parts and duties of it, out of love to God, and to the souls of his people.

11. [Whether he try to avoid the subtle sins of] rash anger, and vain-glory, and covetousness, and love of this world. . . .

12. If he . . . lives in peace with his brethren and flock.[2]

---

[1] *Inverness and Dingwall*, p. 48.
[2] *Works*, II, 442–4.

Catechizing was the continuation of a pre-Restoration practice. There was probably a good deal of variation in the frequency with which that duty was fulfilled. In 1664 the Synod of St Andrews ordered that ministers should catechize on one day of the week, except in seed-time and harvest. Leighton recommended much the same to his clergy in 1669, "onelie seed tyme and harvest being excepted". The Presbytery of Coupar Angus expected its members to catechize at least twice a year, while the Synod of Aberdeen (1667) expected all the people of a parish to be catechized once a year.[1]

Although many of the visitation records have been destroyed, those that are available indicate that the parish clergy of the Restoration Church fulfilled their duties with a remarkably high degree of fidelity and a real awareness of their responsibilities as ministers of God. In a time when clerical immorality would hardly go unnoticed, there are remarkably few charges made against the ministers of the Church.

On 3 February 1664 the Presbytery of Alford resolved to have the next meeting "at the Kirk of Kennethmont, for the trying of a flagrant scandall which was fleeing abroad upon Mr Robt. Cheyne, minister their, that hee should have caused lead his cornes in Octr. last, upon the Lord's day in the evening". To lead the corns, or to load and carry grain to shelter in a cart on the Sabbath day before sundown, was a violation of ecclesiastical discipline, and the trial on 2 March was attended by a large number of witnesses. At the trial it became clear that Mr Cheyne had not led the corns and had in fact "forbade them to lead, and said he hade rather corne should go with the water, and that he went away from them . . .". The culprit turned out to be the minister's wife, who had borrowed horses, organized the neighbours, and led the corn. Mr Cheyne was declared to be "directly under no guiltieness of the scandall" but lax in the discipline of his family. His wife, who was guilty "by her own confessione", was ordered to make "public professione of repentance for the same upon a Lord's day befor the pulpit".[2]

[1] *Dunkeld*, II, p. 111.　　　　[2] *Alford*, pp. 37–9.

More serious was the case of Mr John Gordon, Minister of Kilterne, who was accused of being the father of an illegitimate child.[1] The case was considered by the bishop and the Presbytery of Dingwall. It dragged on for some two years; much conflicting evidence was given, and nothing definitely proven against Mr Gordon.

Such cases were quite rare, and an "Episcopalian" writing in 1690 summarized the character of the parish clergy of Scotland with a restraint remarkable for the pamphlets of that age.

> The Church of Scotland, since the Reformation, was never generally so well provided with Pastors; as at the beginning of the present Persecution: 'Tis true, she has sometimes had some Sons; (such as Doctor Forbes, Doctor Baron, &c.) more Eminent for Learning, than perhaps any of the present Generation will pretend to; But what Church is there in the World, wherein every day, extraordinary Lights are to be found? It cannot be denied neither, that there are amongst us some of but ordinary Parts; but in what Church was it ever otherwise? It would be an odd thing, if the poor cold Climate of Scotland could still afford a thousand Augustines or Aquinas's; perhaps too there may be some, who are not so careful to Adorn their Sacred Office with a suitable Conversation, as they ought to be: But what wonder, when Our Saviour himself had one, a Devil, of Twelve in his Retinue? What Country is it where all the Clergy-Men are Saints? And therefore, I say it over again; the Church of Scotland was never so well planted; generally, since the Reformation, as it was a Year ago.[2]

The visitation records of the period give a similar picture of a large group of clergy who were not especially distinguished, but who sought to fulfil their parish duties with a large measure of devotion and faithfulness. On 30 March 1675 the Presbytery of Inverness made a visitation to the parish of Moy. The questions and answers of the elders about their minister, Mr Rorie, were recorded in the presbytery book.

> 1. They were enquired how they were satisfied with there Minrs doctrine, Answered that they were well satisfied yrwith, and edified.

---

[1] See above, p. 45.
[2] *An Account of the Persecution of the Church in Scotland*, p. 43.

2. Beeing enquired if he was zealous and impartiall in discipline, Answered that he was, without respect of persons.

3. . . . if he was frequent in catechizeing, Answered that he used sometimes to catechize, but wished he were more frequent.

4. . . . if he made conscience of visiting the sick in both his parishes, Answered he did qn he was desired.

5. . . . how long since he celebrated the sacat of the Lords Supper, Answered two years ago. Beeing enquired how long befor yt last time, Answered eight years befor; . . .

6. . . . if he used to haunt aile houses to tipple or drink drunk therein, Answered not, bot lived ministeriallie and most soberly alwayes.

7. . . . if he prayed in any of their families qn he lodged with ym be night. Answered he did frequentlie.

8. . . . if he prayed nightlie and daylie in his own familie, Answered to there certayne knowledge he did.

9. . . . if they had a collector for the penalties, Answered they had, bot was illiterat and so could not keep a book.

10. . . . if he and they did lay a restraint upon pypeing, violeing and danceing at Lickwaks, Answered not as yet.

11. [Did he prohibit the receiving of] strangers from other parishes without testimonialls, Answered negatively.

12. . . . if he had an register for discipline, baptisms, marriages, and collectiones for the poor, Answered that they knew of none, and yt they regrate the want of the samen.

Mr Rorie was called in and "the Moderator . . . blessed God for his diligence and ministeriall, painfull walking". He was then warned to catechize more frequently, to celebrate the Lord's Supper once a year, to fill up his session book, to choose a collector who could read and write, to preach on 29 May, and "to discharge danceing, pypeing, and violeing at likwaks . . .".[1]

Such clergymen, living under a disciplinary system which did not hesitate to point out their shortcomings, fulfilled their parish duties, as they understood the same, remarkably well. They were not men of whom the Church need be ashamed.

The minister of a benefice was entitled to stipend, manse and glebe. Serious efforts were made in the seventeenth century to

---

[1] *Inverness and Dingwall*, pp. 51–3.

provide a minimum stipend. An Act of Parliament in 1617 "Anent the Plantation of Kirks" authorized a Commission "with power . . . out of the saidis teyndis of everie parochin, to appoynt and assigne, at thair discretiounes, ane perpetuall local stipend to the ministers present . . . quhair the provisioun is les nor fyve hundreth merkis [28*l. sterling*] of yeirlie rent of money . . .". They could also unite parishes where the benefice of one was insufficient. The maximum stipend which the Commissioners could grant was 1000 marks (55*l.*).[1]

In 1633 the minimum stipend was raised to 800 marks, or 44*l. sterling.* This step was made possible by the drastic reform of ecclesiastical finance which Charles I undertook. Commutation of teinds (or tithes) to a fixed sum of money now became possible. Most important of all, the lords of erection and other nobles who had held the tithes of the spirituality of the abbeys since the Reformation were deprived of the tithes. This new revenue was channelled through the Commission for Valuation of Teinds into the Church. The Commissioners who received the surrendered teinds were authorized "to appoint, modifie and sett downe a constand and locall stipend and maintenance to ilk minister to be payit out of the teinds of ilk parochine . . .; to divide ample and spatious parochines . . . or to unite divers kirks in whole or in pairt to others . . .".[2] It was a valuable and permanent regularization of ecclesiastical property. It also made Charles I exceedingly unpopular with the nobility of Scotland.

The financial reformation of Charles remained in force during the rest of the century. The "Commission for Planting of Kirks and valuation of Teinds" was authorized anew by Parliament on 6 March 1661. They were again empowered to evaluate the teinds where this had not yet been done, and to enlarge, divide, unite, and build churches.[3] On 8 July 1662 all fourteen bishops were made members of this Commission.[4]

In spite of this excellent system many of the parishes did not reach the 800-mark minimum. At the visitation of Kinethmoth

---

[1] *Dunkeld,* II, 115.
[2] *Source Book of Scottish History,* III, 76.
[3] *Acts of Parliament,* VII, 48.
[4] Ibid., p. 384.

on 9 June 1674 the minister "declaired his stipend yeirly to be three hundreth merks of money [and] three chalder of victuall".[1] A chalder of victual was usually worth 100 marks, and Mr Cheyne's total stipend was 600 marks. At the visitation of Banff in 1683, it was reported that the "allocat stipend . . . is 350 merks of money 3 chalder and a half of victuall".[2]

Moreover, it was sometimes difficult to collect the legal stipend. On 29 March 1671 the Minister of Doores reported that

> He had no mantenance among ym, nor culd he gete so much of his own stipend as would carry him through ye parish to manage his Masters affairs, but was keeped as a poor mendicant ever since he came amongst that people; that they had no inclinaon to doe him the least duty herein, though he had sought after it in the most peaceable manner yt could be, as if, chameleon-like, he could live upon ye aire.[3]

On 5 September 1671 the same presbytery reported that Mr Duncan McCullach, Minister of Vrchart, is "a reproach to ye ministrie and ye Parish in going with so beggerly a habit". However, it was recognized that "much off his stipend be areasted in ye parishoners hands", and Mr McCullach, when asked about his elders and gentlemen, replied that "he had neyr countenance nor maintenance among ym".[4] In 1682 the Minister of Weem complained to the Presbytery of Dunkeld that although "he was presented by the laird of Weem to the whol viccarage and personage, nevertheless he gott but 504 merks . . .".[5]

By Act of Parliament, 25 January 1661, those ministers who had suffered during the late troubles were entitled to apply to the Privy Council for compensation. The funds from vacant stipends were allocated for this purpose.[6] The Privy Council records contain many cases of ministers who applied for this grant. Usually the sum granted was 100*l. sterling*, or sometimes 150*l. sterling*.[7]

The minister of a parish was also entitled to a manse. In 1612

---

[1] *Alford*, p. 216.   [2] *Banff*, II, 53.   [3] *Inverness and Dingwall*, p. 9.
[4] Ibid., pp. 12–13.   [5] *Dunkeld*, I, 442.   [6] *Acts of Parliament*, VII, 18.
[7] *Domestic Annals*, II, 280–81.

Parliament required the minister himself to build and maintain the manse. Such a manse was the property of the minister, and he was entitled to receive the value of the manse from his successor. Moreover, a man did not have to vacate his manse until he had received payment for it.[1]

This system placed a heavy financial burden upon an incoming minister, and in 1649 Parliament required the heritors of each parish to build a manse which would be worth not less than 500 marks nor more than 1000*l. scots*. The minister was required to keep it in repair at his own expense during his incumbency. The Rescissory Act of 1661 repealed the Act of 1649, but in 1663 the Act of 1649 was revived by Parliament.

The latter system was obviously preferable, at least from the point of view of the Church. Efforts were made to require the heritors to purchase those manses which were owned by ministers, thus "freeing" the manse to the parish. In 1661 Mr John Nicolson, Minister of Meigle, purchased the manse from Margret Campbell, the widow of his predecessor, for 1000 marks. When he was transferred to Errol, Bishop Guthrie of Dunkeld, who was also the Minister of Meigle, purchased the manse for 2000 marks, and on 7 April 1670 sold it to the heritors of Meigle for 1000*l. scots*. Whereupon the bishop declared

> that the said manse of Meigill is, and shall be in all tyme coming, a free manse, and both my selfe during my tyme, and others that succeeds in the possessione of the said manse of Meigill . . . shall be oblidged to uphold the said manse during ther possessione therof upon ther owne proper charges and expenses.[2]

In 1664 the Synod of Aberdeen urged "the present incumbentis in the severall churches within this Diocie [to] persue for executione of the Act of parliament relating to the freeing of their manses. . .".[3]

In the various transactions which affected the manse, an accurate appraisal of its worth was frequently necessary. Such an appraisal was ordered by the bishop, attended by members of

---

[1] *Dunkeld*, II, 112–13.   [2] Ibid., I, 182.   [3] *Alford*, p. 53.

presbytery, as well as heritors of the parish, and conducted by workmen who were "solemnly sworn for their faithfulnes".[1] The records of these commissions are accurate indications of the value of manses of the period. The various manses in the Presbyteries of Dunkeld, Coupar Angus, and Meigle ranged in value from 306*l.* scots (25*l. sterling*) to 1395*l.* scots (116*l. sterling*), while the average value was 500–600*l.* scots (42–50*l. sterling*).[2] The manses, like many other houses of the period, reflected the relative poverty of the country. Like the kirks, they were long and low, usually made of clay, turf, and stone, and thatched with heather. On 30 August 1666 the manse of Keig was valued at 369*l. 3s. 8d.* by a commission appointed by Bishop Scougal. The main house consisted of a hall with a chamber at one end and a cellar at the other. There was also a kitchen with a chamber on the end of it. A small stable and a barn were the only other major buildings.[3] The manse of Auchendore was somewhat more adequate. It consisted of a house with stone to the height of the door, with "a timber cellar and a loft above it", an inner chamber with a kitchen in one end, an outer chamber with a study in the end of it "having two windowes, hewen, glassed and cased", and "two fixed beds joyned to the . . . wall". A stable, a barn, and "ane brewing house" completed the major buildings. The whole was valued at 714 marks.[4]

The absence of a manse was not infrequent. In the Presbytery of Inverness there was no manse in Dores or Kiltarlity in 1671, while as late as 1678 there was no manse in Daviot or Moy.[5]

Ministers were also entitled to a glebe of at least four acres, mosse (fuel), and grass for a horse and two cows. The right to four acres was recognized by the Act of Annexation in 1587,[6] and Parliament in 1663 granted the addition to the glebes of grass for a horse and two cows.[7] Since the minister needed his horse to travel to the frequent meetings of presbytery and synod, parishioners often assisted in working the glebe lands, at least at crucial times

---

[1] *Alford.*, p. 98.   [2] *Dunkeld*, II, 114.   [3] Ibid., p. 98.
[4] *Alford*, p. 323. For other examples, see *Alford*, p. 347; *Dunkeld*, I, 468.
[5] *Inverness and Dingwall*, pp. 9, 13, 14, xvi.
[6] *Source Book of Scottish History*, III, 47.   [7] *Dunkeld*, II, 115.

in the year. In 1665 some of the ministers of the Presbytery of
Alford complained of their parishioners, who because of some

> misunderstand and animositie against their ministers . . . did
> withdraw from their assistance . . . from such labors as is usuall
> for parishioners to help their ministers with, such as laboring their
> glebes, and leading their fewell, therefor the brethren thought it
> convenient to refer the said regrat to the Diocesian Synod . . . and
> that, considering that the laws do provide no more grasse for minis-
> ters, but as much as well serve two cows and a horse, wherby they
> cannot publickly performe these labors themselves.[1]

On 20 April 1676 the Synod of Aberdeen began a pension fund
for "the relicks [widows] and children of manie ministers". The
fund was "cordiallie approved and entertained" by the synod.
Each minister was to pay a hundredth part of his annual stipend
to the fund. The fund continued at least until 1688. A similar one
was started in Edinburgh. No evidence has come to light of such
funds existing in other areas.[2]

In spite of the excellent reforms of Charles I, the stipends of
many clergy were still small, and the manses were, at best, quite
modest dwellings.

The restoration of episcopacy in 1661 also meant the technical
restoration of archdeacons, deans, and chapters. Often, though
not invariably, such positions were attached to particular parishes.
A good example is the reconstitution of the Chapter of Argyll by
Act of Parliament, 7 August 1662. The King, with the advice of
the bishop,

> nominates and appoints the persons who are or shall hapen to be
> incumbent in the benefices following viz. the Minister of Loch-
> gaylsheid to be Archdeacon, the minister of Kilmaluage in Lismoir
> to be Dean, the Minister at Dunnoune to be Treasurer, the Minister
> of Kilmichaell in Glastrie to be Chancellour, the Minister at Kil-
> morrew in Croignes to be Chanter, the Minister at Kilmakcharnick
> in Knobdaill to be of the chapter . . .[3]

The income from such dignities was not large. The Dean of
Dunkeld was entitled to receive rent from nine estates—the total

---

[1] *Alford*, pp. 68–9.   [2] Ibid., p. 262, see also Note 28, p. 414.
[3] *Acts of Parliament*, VII, 390.

rent amounted to 93*l. scots* (8*l. sterling*).[1] Moreover, the duties of those appointed to such positions were quite nominal. Robert Leighton, in his *Defence of Moderate Episcopacy*, argued that although the covenants rejected the English prelacy, with "deans, archdeacons, etc.", yet it did not reject a moderate or parochial episcopacy. He went on to add that

> though there is in Scotland at present the name of dean and chapter and commissaries; yet that none of these do exercise at all any part of the discipline under that name, neither any other, as chancellor or surrogate etc., by delegation from bishops, with total exclusion of the community of presbyters from all power and share in it, which is the greatest point of difference between that model and this with us.[2]

In the Presbytery of Dingwall, Mr John Macra was moderator, and although Mr John Mackenzie was the archdeacon, he seems to have participated in the presbytery meetings much as any other presbyter.[3]

As in previous periods, violations of appropriate clerical dress occurred. After the Reformation, Scottish clergy "clothed themselves in hodden grey, wore coloured neckerchiefs, and gowns of blue serge".[4] The Highland clergy especially tended to violate this practice. In 1624 the Synod of Moray reported that "the brethren haunts the Presbytrie with uncomly habits, such as bonats, plaides; whairfor the Assembly ordaines them not to haunt the Presbytrie any mair with uncomly habits".[5] The problem continued after the Restoration. In 1662 it was ordered "by the Bishope [of Aberdeen] with consent of the brethren of the Synod, that the habit of ministers sall be such as beseemeth comeliness, decencie, gravitie, and suitablenes to ther calling, and particularlie in having a cassock coat".[6] In 1671 the Presbytery of Inverness recorded that "Mr Rodericke McKenzie was ordained to goe in a ministeriall habite whan he went to set about any pairt

---

[1] *Dunkeld*, I, 260.   [2] *Works*, v, 80.
[3] *Inverness and Dingwall*, p. 306.
[4] *Alford*, p. xxxii.
[5] Ibid., pp. xxxii–xxxiii.   [6] *Alford*, p. 6.

of his [work]".[1] In 1663 the Synod of Aberdeen made their directions more specific:

> that ministers, masters of Schooles and Universities, and Students of Divinitie be grave in their apperall, it is herby ordained that they use apperall beseeming their degrees, and abstaine from all lyght and new fangled garments in colour or fashion, no wayes beseeming the gravitie of their persounes and paces, and in particular that they have not powdered or long hair, varietie or multitude of ribbons, varietie in their linnens.[2]

It has been customary to bring serious charges against the established clergy in the south-west, the so-called "Western Curates" or "bishop's curates". The Act of Glasgow in 1662 required the south-western clergy either to conform to the settlement or to vacate their parishes. A large majority did not conform, and these men were replaced by clergy largely brought from other parts of Scotland. The total number of replacements necessary was large—almost three hundred. This was about one-third of the entire clergy of the Church of Scotland. Replacement on such a scale would strain the resources of any Church.

The western clergy have been spoken of as unqualified, uneducated, and even illiterate and immoral. A presbyterian pamphlet in 1690 declared that they were "void of all Piety, having entered upon the Ministry with no other Design, but as Men do upon an ordinary Calling, to get a Livelihood".[3] Kirkton wrote that they were

> a crew of young curats . . . and these . . . almost wholly out of the north countrey, where they [the bishops] found a sort of young lads, unstudied and unbred . . . and so profane and void of conscience themselves, that they believed there was none in any other. . . . I take the Lord to witness, I've heard the curats upon Edinburgh streets swear as fast as ever I heard a debaucht red-coat. . . . Of drunkenness I need not accuse them; no man will deny they wallowed in our gutters drunk in their canonical gowns. . . . I am weary of their scandals.[4]

[1] *Inverness and Dingwall*, p. 11. [2] *Alford*, p. 34.
[3] *A brief and true account* . . . , p. 20.
[4] *Scotch Diaries and Memoirs*, pp. 247–8.

The accusation was seconded by Gilbert Burnet.

> The new incumbents, who were put in the places of the ejected preachers . . . were the worst preachers I ever heard: they were ignorant to a reproach: and many of them were openly vicious. They were a disgrace to orders, and the sacred functions; and were indeed the dreg and refuse of the northern parts.[1]

The Earl of Tweeddale also spoke of the western curates as "insufficient scandalous imprudent young fellows",[2] but their opposition to the Accommodation Scheme, which he strongly supported, may account in part for his judgement.

However, there are some indications that the quality of the new curates was not quite as disreputable as these accounts assert. When Leighton became Commendator of Glasgow in 1670, he appointed a commission to try all clergy accused of scandalous behaviour. The commission was empowered to "receive complaints, regulate the affairs of ministers, convene before them the scandalous and unworthy, make trial of what was laid to their charge". The Council of Glasgow appointed the provosts of Glasgow and Ayr, and four other gentlemen, to meet with the commission "and countenance and assist them, and be careful that their orders and citations be obeyed".[3] An "Episcopalian" pamphlet in 1690 referred to this commission. "And yet after all that how many were found worthy of Deposition? Only one (as I am told) of some hundreds; and he too, not without great suspicions of Injustice."[4] Wodrow specified three cases, said that he knew of no other, and implied that the investigation was prejudiced, for "everybody knew that while the bishop was at Dunblane, he had as scandalous and ignorant a clergy as in Scotland, and yet there, he never offered to turn one of them out".[5]

The sober pages of Scott's *Fasti* likewise give a very different picture of the age and academic qualifications of the clergy in the

[1] *Scotch Diaries and Memoirs*, p. 283.   [2] *Lauderdale Papers*, II, 207.
[3] Wodrow, *History*, II, 176.
[4] *An Account of the Present Persecution*, p. 47.
[5] *History*, II, 176.

west. An arbitrary selection of the first three parishes in the Presbytery of Glasgow reveals the following:

Parish of Cadder. In 1664 William Forbes replaced Thomas Melvill, who was deprived. William Forbes was the son of Alexander Forbes, Minister of Campsie. Educated at Marishal College, Aberdeen; M.A. (1656); was granted 100*l.* *sterling* in 1661 for his sufferings during the Interregnum; presented by Charles II to Cadder on 2 March 1664.

Parish of Campsie and Anternomy. In 1662 Archibald Dennistoun replaced John Law, who was deprived. Mr Dennistoun was educated at the University of Glasgow; M.A. (26 July 1637); ordained in 1649 but deposed by the Synod in 1655, "he being of the Resolutionists". He received 100*l.* *sterling* from Parliament in 1661 and was restored to Campsie and Antermony in 1662.

Parish of Carmunnock. In 1665 Robert Boyd replaced Andrew Morton, who was deprived. He was educated at the University of Glasgow; M.A. (1648). Admitted on 18 January 1665, he was a great informer against his parishioners and was ejected from his manse by some of them at the Revolution.[1]

The late Canon J. A. MacCulloch recently made an investigation of the conforming clergy of the south-west. His conclusion was that

of the clergy ordained during the period, if we confine our attention to the south-west (Glasgow, Ayr, Dumfries, and Galloway), eighty-one were ordained to fill vacant charges in 1662 and soon after, and of these thirty were graduates of Edinburgh, twenty-five were graduates of Glasgow, nine were graduates of St Andrews, and fifteen were graduates of Aberdeen. . . . Those clergy ordained in 1662 or succeeding years were no younger than Presbyterian ministers of the period when ordained.[2]

It is clear that the "curates" were at least technically qualified and not guilty of gross immorality. Most of them had completed their university training and taken their trials. Most were not ministers of parishes, but schoolmasters and tutors.[3] They probably represented a lower quality of clergy who, for one reason or

---

[1] *Fasti*, III, 373, 376, 379.   [2] Quoted in Goldie, *Short History*, pp. 24–5.
[3] Henderson, *Religious Life in Seventeenth-Century Scotland*, p. 178.

another, did not receive a benefice until the large number of vacancies occurred in 1661–2. Their parishioners were an exceedingly difficult group to work with, and the curates lived under a perpetual stigma of unpopularity. Most were rabbled at the Revolution.

Gilbert Burnet and five others were sent by Leighton on a tour of the area in 1670 to persuade the people to accept his Accommodation Scheme. Burnet's description of what he found shows something of the difficult situation which the "curates" faced:

> We were indeed amazed to see a poor commonalty so capable to argue upon points of government, and on the bounds to be set to the power of princes in matters of religion. Upon all these topics they had texts of scripture at hand, and were ready with their answers to anything that was said to them. This measure of knowledge was spread even amongst the meanest of them, their cottagers and their servants. They were indeed vain of their knowledge, much conceited of themselves, and were full of a most entangled scrupulosity: so that they found or made difficulties in everything that could be laid before them.[1]

Examples of repression of nonconforming clergy have so frequently been given that it is well to remember that life was not always pleasant for those who conformed. As late as 1685, three groups of clergy in the south-west found it necessary to send letters to the Bishop of Galloway begging his protection from the tumults of the area. The Ministers of Stoneykirk, Kirkmaiden, Portpatrick, Stranraer, Inch, and Soulseat sent a common letter to the bishop. "May it please your Lordshipp We again represent to your L/ our dangerous condition, so that hitherto not with out great hazard of our Lives we have continued in the exercise of our ministrie. . . ."[2]

Even the most distinguished minister who wished to support the Establishment would have found an assignment in the south-west unpleasant. The "curates" failed to commend themselves to the majority of their parishioners. It is probable that no conforming

---

[1] *History*, I, 524–5.
[2] *Miscellany of the Scottish History Society*, III, 94.

clergy could have done so. Yet the "curates" have been too much slandered and "were in no official sense unqualified".[1]

Sometimes the accusations made against the clergy of the south-west have been extended to include the whole body of Restoration clergy. This general indictment is quite unjustified. Canon MacCulloch, who investigated the charges brought against the clergy throughout the whole period, has concluded: "While it is sad that even this comparatively small number of deprivals for drunkenness or immorality should have occurred, they are spread over a period of twenty-nine years, and by no means correspond to the general accusations . . ." often made against them.[2] A Presbyterian historian also affirmed that

> The charges of Immorality and Ignorance, doubtless justified for a time, as regards some of the clergy of the West, were falsely brought against the clergy as a whole. The conclusion appears just that they were made against the clergy as a whole, and continued to be repeated, in that spirit of sectarianism which does not shrink from misrepresentation in order to blacken an opponent and so justify a policy, and that the Episcopal clergy were slandered.[3]

Nor was the Restoration Church lacking in men who would have been outstanding in any age. Gilbert Burnet was Minister of Salton and later Professor of Divinity at the University of Glasgow, before his departure for England. John Cockburn, a nephew of Patrick Scougall, was brought up in the home of the bishop. A presbyter of Aberdeen, he was one of the last in that city to sign the Test Act. He was deprived in 1689 and confined to the Edinburgh Tolbooth for "upwards of half a year". He attended the court of James at St Germain, but was put in prison after refusing to change his religion. In 1698 he was appointed minister of the Episcopal Church at Amsterdam and later Rector of Northolt, Middlesex. He was designated by Queen Anne to be one of the bishops for the American colonies, had that scheme been put into effect.[4]

---

[1] Henderson, op. cit., 178.
[2] Quoted in Goldie, *Short History*, p. 25.
[3] *Dunkeld*, I, 58.   [4] *Fasti*, I, 340.

James Blair, who was educated at the University of Edinburgh, became Minister of Cranstoun in 1679. Deprived in 1681 for not taking the Test, he departed for England. He was sent by the Bishop of London to Virginia in 1685 to complete a well-known and distinguished career.[1]

Lawrence Charteris was a close friend of Leighton and one of the six preachers sent by that prelate to preach in the west for the Accommodation. He became Professor of Divinity at the University of Edinburgh in 1675 and gathered round him a group of young men who, like himself, disliked that royal absolutism which was so conspicuous a feature of the Church.[2] Burnet wrote that he "had great tenderness and was a very perfect friend, and a most sublime Christian. . . . He had read all the lives and the epistles of great men . . . and delighted much in the mystics [and] had read the fathers much. . . . He made religion appear amiable in his whole deportment." [3]

Hugh Rose and James Nairn were noted for their piety; George Garden, his brother James, and Henry Scougall, son of the Bishop of Aberdeen, were exemplars of a tradition of mystical piety which is one of the most attractive aspects of the life of the Restoration Church.[4] Henry Scougall's simple and beautiful *Life of God in the Soul of Man* is probably the finest example of devotional writing in the period. In 1673 the Synod of Aberdeen elected Henry Scougall to be Professor of Divinity "without ane dissassenting voyce".[5] Two years later, Mr Scougall preached in "the Kirk of Old Machar" (Aberdeen) at the opening of synod.[6] The sermon has been preserved and is entitled "Of the Importance and Difficulty of the Ministerial Function".[7] In it the preacher refers to "holy Chrysostom", Gregory Nazianzen, Gregory the Great, Ambrose, Augustine, and "that worthy gentleman, and excellent minister . . . that sweet singer of Israel, Mr. Herbert".

We may conclude that a remarkably high standard of clerical life was maintained throughout the Restoration Church in Scot-

---

[1] *Fasti*, I, 310.   [2] Ibid., p. 360.   [3] Burnet, *History*, I, 385.
[4] See below, p. 160.   [5] *Alford*, p. 203.   [6] Ibid., p. 231.
[7] *Works*, p. 276 ff.

land. Educational standards were not lax and candidates under-
went an examination which was a very thorough one. The clergy
shared in the general poverty of much of the country, but were at
the same time released from the whole system of wealthy benefices
with absentee incumbents which was so well known in the
southern kingdom.[1]

Their duties as well as their lives were shaped by the traditions
and standards of the Church of Scotland. The three ministerial
duties which Henry Scougall selected for his sermon were catechizing, preaching, and administering discipline. It was especially
in their performance of the last duty that we are most conscious
of the previous traditions of Scotland. It has always been a duty
of parish clergy to preach the Word and to catechize the faithful.
The administration of the sacraments was not very frequent in
Scotland, and clergy were frequently remiss in celebrating the
Lord's Supper regularly.[2] But it was especially in their administration of discipline through public admonition, kirk-session, and
presbytery, that the clergy of the Church of Scotland showed most
clearly that continuity of the presbyterian disciplinary system
which was so conspicuous a part of Church life during the Restoration period. It was not easy to administer discipline well. Scougall
wrote that "Discipline is an edged tool, and they had need be no
fools that meddle with it".[3] It was at least administered with
faithfulness and zeal, and continued to be one of the important
duties of the parish clergy of the Church of Scotland throughout
the Restoration.

    [1] Morer wrote: "They [the clergy in Scotland] have a greater Equality in
their Benefices than the Clergy of England, few exceeding 100*l*. Sterling, and
as few below 20*l*. So that as the first Stipend will hardly allow 'em to live great
the other is not so mean in that cheap Kingdom, but they may live without
Scandal." *Short Account*, pp. 50–51.
    [2] See below, pp. 140 ff.
    [3] *Works*, p. 290.

6

PARISH LIFE IN THE KIRK

MANY of the medieval parish churches continued to be used after the Reformation. An Englishman who visited Scotland near the end of the seventeenth century described the churches he saw:

> In the Country, they [the churches] are poor and mean, covered no better than their ordinary Cottages. . . . But in the Boroughs and Cities they are Brick'd and Tile'd, and well enough furnished with Gallaries and other Conveniences for the Parishioners. The Precentor's Desk is under the Pulpit, and under him the Stool of Penance, or rather a Bench for five or six to sit on, to be seen by the Congregation, and bear the shame of their Crimes. . . . Chancels they have none, nor Altars. . . .[1]

The typical church was long, narrow, and low. In the middle of the south wall was the pulpit, with the reader's desk below it. Near the pulpit was the pillar or stool of repentance. There were usually two galleries, one in the east and one in the west, often with outside stairways leading up to them. Sometimes there was a gallery in the north side, opposite the pulpit. There were few windows, and these small ones.[2] Visitation reports frequently describe the condition of the church. At Kildrummie (1680) it was "reported that the fabrick of the kirk was in sufficient repair, save what was wanting in the loss of some heather . . .".[3] The Bishop of Moray and the Presbytery of Inverness in 1680 reported that "the fabrick of the Church [of Kirkhill] was found compleit in thack, glass windowes, lofts, desks, church bible, pulpit cloath, and an excellent Bell and bellhouse",[4] while at Petty, "the

---

[1] Morer, *Short Account*, p. 53.
[3] Ibid., p. 315.
[2] *Alford*, pp. xvi–xvii.
[4] *Inverness and Dingwall*, p. 109.

Fabrick of the Church is compleit and plenishit dayly with Lofts and dasks and other things necessary".[1]

However, many of the reports were not so encouraging. In 1665 Mr Murdoch McKenzie, Minister at Lochbroome, told the Presbytery of Dingwall that "he has not a convenient meeting place for preaching, the Kirk of Lochbroom being unthatched". [2] In 1681 the members of the Presbytery of Dingwall noted that "their Churches were werie ruinous".[3] If the situation at Killichrist is typical, they had good reason to complain. In 1682 Mr George Cumin and his brother were accused before the Presbytery of Dingwall of "putting some oxen [in the Kirk of Killichrist] and encloseing ym ytin over night". However, when the two brothers appeared before Presbytery,

> they answered yt they did not put anie of yr cattel into ye church, but yt some beasts of theirs yt feeding about yt Kirkyard . . . did stragle into ye church, which had neiyr doore nor roofe. . . .[4]

The Presbytery of Inverness reported (1682) that "the Fabrick of the Church [of Croy] being considered, and some defect ruin found in thack and windowes, [it] was recommended to the Minister and Elders to looke carefull to its reparation". The next day a visitation at Daviot reported: "In regard the Church was found ruinous, wanting thack in severall places, the windowes not glassed, the Lo. Bishop seriously recommended to their [the Minister and elders] care to have this helped with all convenient speed." [5]

The poor condition of church buildings and manses in Scotland is only part of a general picture. In 1661 an English naturalist, John Ray, made a short trip through Scotland. He wrote:

> In the best Scottish houses, even the king's palaces, the windows are not glazed throughout, but the upper part only, the lower have two wooden shuts or folds to open at pleasure and admit fresh air. . . . The ordinary country houses are pitiful cots, built of stone, and

---

[1] *Inverness and Dingwall*, p. 110.   [2] Ibid., p. 309.
[3] Ibid., p. 344.   [4] Ibid., p. 347.
[5] Ibid., pp. 105-6.

covered with turves, having in them but one room, many of them no chimneys, the windows very small holes and not glazed.[1]

Many of the parish churches were undoubtedly in very poor condition, but so were many other buildings of the time.

There were no pews inside the church. Heritors and other gentlemen received permission to build their own "desks" or pews (it is not certain whether these were square pews), while others brought chairs or stools with them for the long services. The Kirk-Session of Elgin (December 1661) granted "license to Mr. Thomas Gordoune, doctor of phisik, to build ane loaft above Mr. John Douglas desk on the south syd of the church above the doore that enters into the session house, seeing God hes castne his lot be providence to live within this burgh".[2] In 1665 the Presbytery of Alford received a request from Robert Smith, who "hade lately putt up a new desk" in the Church of Auchindeor and who sought permission "either to transport his desk from that church to another, or to sell the same to any within the parish who wold be pleased to buy it". The request was "thought reasonable" and granted.[3] In 1678 a statement was deposited with the same presbytery by George Garioch, who having had his desk for forty years, now gave it to William Garioch, his brother's son.[4]

Presbyteries often dealt with disputes over desks. In 1670 "there was a complaint given in [to the Presbytery of Alford] by James and John Gordones, against Thomas, Robert, and Alaster Stuarts, for violently removing a dask belonging to them, utering minaceing speeches on the Lord's day in defense of that deed". They were rebuked by the presbytery.[5] Sometimes more drastic action was necessary. In 1664 Alexander Burnet, Bishop of Aberdeen, ordered a complete reassignment of space in the Kirk of Towy. On the appointed day members of presbytery and the

---

[1] *Domestic Annals*, II, 283. In 1679 Thomas Kirke, a Yorkshire squire, published a *Modern Account of Scotland*. His exaggerations are probably not far from the truth. "The houses of the commonality are very mean, mudwall and thatch the best. But the poorer sort live in such miserable huts as never eye beheld; men, women, and children pig together in a poor mousehole of mud, heath, and such-like matter. . . ." *Domestic Annals*, II, 407.

[2] *Elgin*, II, 301. See also p. 303.   [3] *Alford*, p. 68.
[4] Ibid., p. 296.   [5] Ibid., p. 156.

people of the parish were present and the space within the church carefully assigned "to John Forbes of Towy from the fourth couple in the South side to the East side of the East door; to Williame Farqrsoune of Mill of Towy from the West side of the East doore four couples Westward . . .", etc.[1]

The most striking thing about the public services of the Restoration Church was their continuity with the worship of the preceding presbyterian era. A few changes were introduced, and these have some importance, but the general pattern and character of daily and Sunday services were largely unaltered. Sir George MacKenzie wrote in 1691 about "Scotland during the REIGN of King Charles II":

> The Reader will be astonished, when we inform him; that the way of Worship in our Church, differed nothing from what the Presbyterians themselves practised, (except only that we used the Doxologie, the Lord's Prayer, and in Baptism, the Creed, all which they rejected.) We had no Ceremonies, Surplice, Altars, Cross in Baptisms, nor the meanest of those things which would be allowed in England by the Dissenters, in way of Accommodation:[2]

The same point was made by the author of *The Case of the Present Afflicted Clergy in Scotland Truly Represented* (1690):

> . . . As to the Worship, it's exactly the same both in the Church and Conventicle; in the Church there are no Ceremonies at all injoyned or practised, only some Persons more reverent, think fit to be uncovered which our Presbyterians do but by halves even in the time of Prayer; we have no Liturgy nor Form of Prayer, no not in the Cathedrals, the only difference in this point is, our Clergy are not so overbold nor fulsome in their extemporary Expressions as the others are . . . and we generally conclude one of our Prayers with that which our Saviour taught and commanded, which the other Party decry as Superstitious and Formal; Amen too gives great Offence, tho neither the Clerk nor People use it, only the Minister sometimes shuts up his Prayer with it. The Sacraments are Administered after the same Way and Manner by both; neither so much as kneeling at the Prayers, or when they receive the Elements of the Lord's Supper, but all sitting together at a long Table in the Body

---

[1] *Alford*, pp. 69–71.　　　　[2] *Vindication*, p. 9.

of the Church or Chancel. In Baptism neither Party use the Cross, nor are any Godfathers or Godmothers required, the Father only promising for his Child.[1]

The changes made were authorized by synodical action. At its first meeting in October 1662 the Synod of Edinburgh ordered:

> . . . item, that the Lordis prayer sould be repeited, once by the minister at every preaching, or twyse as the minister pleased; item, that the Doxologie or "Glorie to the Father", being a song composed and universallie sung in the church quhen the Arianes and uther sectis denyed the deitie of Our Saviour, that the same be agane revived and sung, . . . item, that the Belieff or Apostles creed be repeited at the Sacrament of baptisme, by the father of the chyld, or by the minister at his discretione. . . .[2]

At the Restoration there was probably a good deal of suspicion that more radical changes would be made, and indeed these may well have been considered. In December 1663 Alexander Brodie wrote in dismay that "I heard that the Bishop, Michel of Aberden, was Arminian; that he had injoyed priuat baptism and communion, and spok something of the necessiti of Baptism; that the Bishop of M[oray] had drawen al the peopl to kneel at the com-

---

[1] *The Case of the Present Afflicted Clergy*, preface. In 1677 Bishop Paterson of Galloway wrote about "the worship practised in this church, *it being notourly the same, without variation, as it was under Presbytery*". MSS. Episcopal Chest, B.8; quoted in Stephen, *Life of Sharp*, p. 503. The author of *An Account of the Present Persecution of the Church in Scotland* (1690) made the same point: "We still maintain'd what themselves [the nonconformists held]: the same Articles of Faith; we worshipped God after the same manner: there is no imaginable Difference between Them and Us in the Administration of Sacraments. . . . All that was ever controverted amongst us, was the Point of Church-Government; 'tis true, we use the Lord's Prayer and the Doxology, and commonly require the Creed in Baptism, which they do not: if these can justifie a Separation, we are guilty . . .", p. 11.

[2] Nicoll, pp. 380–81. Sentiment for episcopacy was strongest in the Aberdeen area, yet the injunctions of that synod were similar to those of other synods: " . . . the Reader sall begin with a set forme of prayer, especiallie with the Lord's Prayer, and therafter they ar to read some psalmes, with some chapteris of the Old Testament, therafter they are to rehearse the Apostolick creed publicklie, and in rehearsing of it to stand up, afterward that they read some chapteris of the New Testament according to the appoyntment of the respective ministers, and last of all they are to rehearse the Ten Commandments publickly; . . ." *Alford*, p. 1.

munion. Thus does corruption insensibili creip in, and will over-
spread, if the Lord prevent not". Two days later, on 25 December,
he wrote that "I heard that the Bishop had ministred the communion kneiling, and that the peopl had gon alongst with him".[1]

Moreover, in those tumultuous times, even minor matters often
became points of great controversy. This was clearly recognized
by Leighton:

> This one word I shall add, That this difference should arise to a
> great height, may seem somewhat strange to any man, that calmly
> considers, that there is in this church no change at all, neither in the
> doctrine nor worship; no, nor in the substance of the discipline
> itself; but when it falls on matter easily inflammable, a little sparkle,
> how great a fire will it kindle! [2]

Nevertheless, to an outsider the changes in public worship would
seem very minor indeed, and one may well sympathize with the
English nonconformist student at Glasgow in 1672 who wrote:

> The public worship in the churches, though the Archbishop him-
> self preach, is in all respects after the same manner managed as in
> the Presbyterian congregations in England, so that I much wondered
> why there should be any dissenters here, till I came to be informed
> of the renunciation of the Covenant enjoined, and the imposition
> of the hierarchy. [3]

On the other hand, the above quotations do show that some
changes were made, and a complete list of alterations would
include more than the Doxology, Creed and Lord's Prayer. It
seems clear that the reason for all these Restoration developments
was a desire to revive public services as they had been known in
the earlier part of the seventeenth century and before the late
rebellion. Those elements of worship which had developed during
the period of the Covenants were dropped or forbidden, while
earlier practices which had been abandoned were now revived.

The Westminster *Directory* was widely used in Scotland during
the Interregnum—in 1646 the Synod of Moray reported that

---

[1] *Diaries of the Lairds of Brodie*, pp. 394–5.
[2] "A Defence of Moderate Episcopacy", *Works*, v, 78.
[3] Butler, *Life and Letters of Leighton*, p. 486.

almost all churches were using it.[1] The first Restoration Synod of Aberdeen ordered that "the Directorie practized by order of the late illegall Assemblie be layd assyd, and not made use of in tyme coming".[2] The Church tended to turn to the old Knoxian *Book of Common Order*, or "Psalm Book" for guidance. Thus the same synod ordered that for daily prayers "the liturgie in the old Psalm Book be practised".[3]

Another early tradition revived at the Restoration was the office of the "Reader" and the development of the "reader's service". The office of Reader is referred to in the *First Book of Discipline*, which enacted that "in the Churches where no minister can be had presently, must be appointed the most apt men that distinctly can read the Common Prayers and the Scriptures".[4] In the early part of the seventeenth century readers were quite common. A first bell called the people to church, and the ringing of the second bell signified the beginning of the service. The reader was in charge until the third bell rang. He conducted a service mainly of psalms and lessons. In 1641 the Kirk-Session of Oldmachar gave instruction to the reader to "begin his reading precisely at the end of the second bell, and then to read a chapter and thereafter to sing two verses of a psalm and immediately thereafter the catechesis to be said and then . . . to read till the minister come to the pulpit . . .".[5]

The Westminster *Directory* dispensed with readers, and about 1645 the old reader's service of psalms and lessons was displaced in many areas by the lecture system. Lectures "to explain the Scripture and give some short notes on it" were at first weekday exercises. But "at lenth finding it a more considerable work than at first they reponed . . . it fell in disuse and lectures on the sabbath fornoon came in the room of it".[6]

---

[1] Quoted in Henderson, *Religious Life*, p. 7.   [2] *Alford*, p. 2.

[3] In the seventeenth century, the *Book of Common Order* was published under the title, "The Psalmes of David in Meter, with the Prose, wherevnto is added Prayers commonly vsed in the Kirk", 1611 (Spott's edition, 1868).

[4] *Source Book of Scottish History*, II, 162.

[5] MSS. Kirk Session Minutes, quoted in Henderson, op. cit., p. 7.

[6] Wodrow, *Analecta*, II, 291.

The abandonment of lessons and the sung psalter was not popular, and a revival of the singing of metrical psalms took place even before the Restoration. In 1653 John Nicoll wrote:

> It wald be rememberit that, in the yeir of God 1645, the reiding of chapteris in the kirk by the commoun reidar, and singing of psalmes wer dischargit, and in place thairof come in the lectureis, quhid indured till the incuming of the Englische airmy. This did not content the pepill, because thair wes no reiding of chapteris nor singing of psalmes on the Saboth day; quhairfoir the minsteris thocht it guid to restoir the wonted custome of singing of psalmes, as als the exercise of the catechisme.[1]

However, it was not until the Restoration that the old service was fully restored. The office of Reader was revived, and the reading of lessons as well as the metrical psalter enjoined. Nicoll wrote that

> . . . the singing of Psalmes wes broght in agane in the kirkes of Edinburgh in the begyning of October 1653; and now this yeir 1662, the reiding of Scriptures wes of new broght in agane and the Psalmes sung with this additioun, "Glorie to the Father, to the Sone, and to the Holy Ghost". This now brocht in by autoritie of the Bischops with greater devotioun than evir befoir, for all the pepill rais at the singing, "Glorie to the Father. . . ."[2]

The restoration of Readers was authorized by the Bishop and Synod of Aberdeen in 1662, when it was enacted "that there sall be Readers of the Scriptures in every congregatione".[3] In 1663 the Presbytery of Fordyce recorded an agreement which indicates the duties expected of a Reader, who in this case was the schoolmaster, Mr William Mair:

> He sall lykwayes reid the comone prayeris and chapteris devoitlie tuyes ilk weik day, viz., morneing and evineing, within the kirk of the said burghe, and for that effect sall cum in to the said kirk immediatlie efter the ringing of bell sall ceis, and on the Sabothe in the morneing and siclyk betuixt the second and thrid bell befornoon and efternoon sall reid and say the prayeris and sall tak up the psalme within the said kirk at all occasionis necessar, and as he salbe requyrit.[4]

---

[1] Nicoll, pp. 114–15.   [2] Ibid., p. 382.
[3] *Alford*, p. 1.   [4] *Banff*, II, 39.

The reason for the revival of the "reader" which took place at the Restoration is quite clear—to return to that pattern of worship which existed before the late troubles began. James Sharp, in his directions to the Synod of St Andrews in 1662, "did signifie to the brethren that it's His Majestie's will that henforth the way of worship prescribed by the Directory should ceas, and that the former way of reading Scriptur befor sermon by readers, where they may be had, be used".[1]

The Creed, Lord's Prayer and Doxology are usually called the distinctive features of Restoration worship. Yet these three practices were all revivals of earlier traditions. The Lord's Prayer occurs in Knox's *Book of Common Order*[2] and was used regularly until the period of the Covenants.[3] The Apostles' Creed was part of Calvin's catechism, and the whole of the catechism was included in the *Book of Common Order*.[4] The Doxology was also well known prior to the late rebellion.[5] Thus even those items which distinguish most conspicuously the worship of the Restoration Church serve to show its continuity with the earlier traditions of the Church of Scotland.[6]

During the Restoration, the Church of Scotland had no official liturgy or prayer book. The reception accorded the Prayer Book of 1637 precluded any attempt to introduce an authorized service book again. John Cockburn wrote that the bishops were forbidden to introduce canons and a liturgy by orders from Court, "lest such things should provoke to a new Rebellion".[7] The complaints of Gilbert Burnet about the need for a liturgy are eloquent testimony to the lack of one:

> . . . our worship . . . is extremely flat in all the parts of it. Our Church prayers are long without any order and often very dull. I must say this Church the only one in the world which hath no rule

---

[1] *Dunkeld*, I, 60.
[2] *Book of Common Order*, p. 102 (Spott's edition, 1868).
[3] Henderson, op. cit., pp. 102-3.
[4] *Book of Common Order*, pp. 217-19.
[5] Henderson, op. cit., pp. 148-9.
[6] For the same pattern in the conduct of funerals, see below, p. 149 f.
[7] *Miscellany of the Scottish History Society*, II, 354.

for worship. Even the Presbyterians had their directory. How heavy and grievous must it be yt all the prayers of the Church depend upon the extemporary gift of the minister? the compiling of a grave lyturgie, the prayers whereof shall be short and Scriptural and fitly depending one upon another, should be no inconsiderable service to the Church.[1]

However, there are signs that a few individuals and groups were conscious of the values of an ordered liturgy and desirous of its introduction into Scotland. According to Burnet, this was one of Leighton's reasons for choosing the see of Dunblane:

When Leighton was prevailed on to accept a bishopric, he chose Dunblane, a small diocese, as well as a little revenue. But the deanery of the chapel royal was annexed to that see. So he was willing to engage in that, that he might set up the common prayer in the king's chapel.[2]

Burnet also claimed to have used the Book of Common Prayer, quoting it from memory, when he was Minister of Saltoun. "I was the only man I heard of in Scotland," he wrote, "that used the forms of Common Prayer, not reading, but repeating them."[3] These two examples are usually regarded as the only cases in Scotland where the Book of Common Prayer was used. However, the Reverend Wm. M'Millan, in his article "The Anglican Book of Common Prayer in the Church of Scotland",[4] has collected a number of other examples. These show clearly that the Prayer Book was occasionally used in several parts of Scotland. Alexander Brodie recorded (1662) that "yesterday the Bishop of Edinburgh [George Wishart] did baptis the Advocat' son, and usd some of the ceremonies, and Service Book. I desird to spread this befor God."[5]

More significant than these isolated instances of actual use was the growing sentiment in some sections for the introduction of a liturgy. In 1665–6 the bishops did in fact consider the possibility of this step. Moreover, a service book was apparently drawn up at

---

[1] *Miscellany of the Scottish History Society*, II, 354–5. [2] *History*, I, 245.
[3] Clarke and Foxcroft, *Life of Burnet*, p. 57.
[4] *Records of the Scottish Church History Society*, IV, 145–7.
[5] *Diaries of the Lairds of Brodie*, p. 270.

this time for possible use. On 5 February 1666 Archbishop Burnet wrote to the Archbishop of Canterbury of their plans: ". . . for our confession it is likely we may approve the articles of the Church of England, but our liturgie doth not please me, and (unlesse it be rectified) I feare will not please others: However, I am for offering all to his Maties view. . . ." [1] "Our liturgy" may have been drawn up in Scotland at this time. A month later, this liturgy had been rejected for another plan. On 8 March Archbishop Burnet wrote:

> Wee have had many debates about our liturgie, and to no great purpose; at last, when it was apparent that our new forms would not please, another booke of common-prayer was produced, which is that our predecessours offered to King Charles the first, and is made wp of the ordinary confession, collects, and other prayers wsed in the Church of England; only the litany and responses are waved; this gave more satisfaction . . . and this with our canons is to be offered to his Matie by my lord St. Andrews some tyme the next moneth. [2]

Apparently the bishops were considering the introduction of the book of 1637, possibly in one of its earlier drafts.

News of the proposals to restore a liturgy aroused opposition, and in September, 1665, eight lairds and gentry were imprisoned by Royal order for opposing the project. However, "these persons wer gentlie and courteouslie usit, and haid libertie to pas to the feildis and pastyme, being, as wes reportit, imprissoned on wrangous informatione; sum alledgeand that thir persones wer set to oppose the Bischops courses in bringing in the Service buik and buik of Cannones, and sum utheris we knaw now quhat till it be reveillit heirafter. God save the King." [3]

The project was dropped, and no attempt was made again to authorize a liturgy for public use. Interest in the Prayer Book did not die, however, and the English book was used in family worship in a number of instances. During the visitation of the University of Edinburgh after the Revolution, Dr Monro, who was on trial,

---

[1] *Lauderdale Papers*, II, Appendix, xxx.
[2] Ibid., p. xxxiii.   [3] Nicoll, p. 439.

roundly declared that "the Book of Common Prayer was read in many Families in Scotland, ever since the Restitution of King Charles II".[1] During the same visitation, Dr John Strachan, Professor of Divinity, also affirmed "that I have indeed made use of the English Service in my Family, as judging it to be the way of Worship most consonant and agreeable to the Word of God, and the practice of the whole Catholick Church . . . it being a most devout and serious way of offering up our Prayers and Praises to Almighty God".[2]

This tendency was given official sanction by the Privy Council in 1680. On 12 February of that year the following resolution was passed:

> The lords of his majesty's privy council, having considered a representation made to them by some of their own number, that divers persons of quality, and others of this kingdom, were very desirous to have the allowance of the use of the solemn form of divine worship, after the laudable and decent custom and order of the church of England, in their private families, do hereby allow of the same, and give assurance to them of the council's countenance and protection therein.[3]

In consequence of this permission, English Prayer Books were sent to Scotland and a number of them were sold. On 2 June 1681 Dr Francis Turner, Chaplain to the Duke of York, then in Edinburgh, wrote to Archbishop Sancroft that "our Common Prayer Bookes do sell (the booksellers tell me) in great numbers at Edenburgh".[4]

Something of the tenor of this movement can be gathered from the letters of the time. In 1685 John Paterson, Bishop of Edinburgh, wrote to Sancroft of his desires: "The formidable rebellion being now utterlie broken in both kingdoms . . . it was verie desirable if the nationall Church could now be so happie as to have devout forms of worship setled therein. . . ."[5] The previous year the Earl of Perth also wrote to Sancroft. "The Doctor

---

[1] *Presbyterian Inquisition*, p. 32. [2] Ibid., p. 79.
[3] Wodrow, *History*, III, 232.
[4] Clarke, *Collection of Letters*, p. 29. [5] Ibid., p. 86.

[Dr Fall, Principal of the College of Glasgow] wil speak to your Grace, too, of getting Common Prayer to be used in the King's house here; it is my Lord Treasurer's motion, and to his care wee owe so good and pious a design. . . ." [1]

This movement was strongest in the diocese of Aberdeen, and in 1683 a committee of the synod was authorized to draw up a small prayer book. In 1685 they reported that their work was almost finished. It consisted of

> . . . some prayers to be used by Kirk Readers in the churches where there are prayers morning and evening, and to be used upon the Lord's day befor reading the Scriptures; . . . also . . . some short petitions or Collects, to be insert and made use of in the said prayers upon some particular occasions. . . . They had noted some places of Scripture which they judged most proper to be read at extraordinary dyets; and . . . a method of reading the holy Scriptures in congregations throwout the year and . . . some forms of prayer to be used in families morning and evening, together with some prayers to be said by children. [2]

There are a few other indications of the movement. James Gordon's *The Reformed Bishop* advocated communion three times a year and a modest liturgy. The work was published in 1679, with later editions in 1680 and 1689. The author's son was one of those most interested in bringing the English liturgy into use in Scotland. Yet he was quite unfamiliar with the actual use of the Prayer Book and found difficulty with the mechanics of a liturgy when he had to read a service in London. "I found my selfe more concerned with that exercise than with both preaching and praying in Scotland without book." [3]

This movement, small and tentative as it was, does clearly show that the development of liturgical worship in Scotland in the eighteenth century had its origins in the Restoration period, when considerable interest, especially in the north, had existed in such a "good and pious design".

Thomas Morer, an English chaplain serving in Scotland at the

---

[1] Clarke, *Collection of Letters*, p. 69.   [2] *Alford*, p. 366.
[3] *Gordon's Diary*, p. 38.

time of the Revolution, has left an excellent description of the public services of the Kirk on Sunday:

> First, The Precentor about half an hour before the Preacher comes, reads two or three Chapters to the Congregation, of what part of Scripture he pleases, or as the Minister gives him Directions. As soon as the Preacher gets into the Pulpit, the Precentor leaves Reading, and sets a Psalm, singing with the People, till the Minister by some Sign orders him to give over. The psalm ended, the Preacher begins, Confessing Sins and Begging Pardon, Exalting the Holiness and Majesty of God, and setting before Him our Vileness and Propensity to transgress His Commandments. Then he goes to Sermon, delivered always by heart . . . The Sermon finsh'd he returns to Prayer; thanks God for that Opportunity to deliver His Word; prays for all Mankind, for all Christians, for that particular Nation, for the Sovereign and Royal Family, without naming any, for Subordinate Magistrates, for Sick People (especially such whose Names the Precentor hands up to him), then concludes with the Lord's Prayer . . . After this another Psalm is sung, named by the Minister, and frequently suited to the Subject of his Sermon; which done, he gives the Benediction, and dismisses the Congregation for that time.
>
> This is the Morning-Service, which being repeated pretty early in the Afternoon (because in the interim they eat nothing) makes up the Lord's Day Duty, as to Publick Worship, saving that they forget not the Poor, who are numerous . . . and so put into the Bason what they think fit, either at their Going in or Coming out, to be disposed of by the Minister and Elders . . .[1]

Synodical instructions to the Reader give a somewhat fuller account of his part of the service.

> . . . the Reader sall begin with a set forme of prayer, especiallie with the Lord's Prayer, and therafter they ar to read some psalmes, with some chapteris of the Old Testament, therafter they ar to rehearse the Apostolick creed publicklie, and in rehearsing of it to stand up, afterward that they read some chapteris of the New Testament according to the appoyntment of the respective ministers, and last of all they are to rehearse the Ten Commandments publickly; . . .[2]

As had been true in the first part of the century, it was not easy to make the Reader's service an integral part of Sunday worship.

---

[1] Morer, *Short Account*, pp. 60–61.   [2] *Alford*, p. 1.

K

A number of people did not attend, and even the minister customarily arrived only at the third bell. As late as 1684 the Synod of Aberdeen "recommended to the bretheren of this Diocess to be present at, and countenance the reading of the holy Scriptures in the respective churches upon the Lord's day befor sermon, that therby their people may be oblidged the more frequentlie to repair to, and more reverently to attend upon the said ordinance".[1] It was said of Henry Scougal that

> He endeavoured to bring them to a devout and constant attendance on the public worship, where he always went, and joined with them at the beginning of it; thinking it very unfit that the invocation of Almighty God, the reading some portions of the Holy Scriptures, making a confession of our Christian faith, and rehearsing the ten commandments, should be looked upon only as a preludium for ushering in the people to the church, and the minister to the pulpit.[2]

Leighton, and those who agreed with him on the need for this kind of reform, did not seek merely to have Holy Scripture read publicly in goodly quantity. There was a deeper motive—the desire for a solemn and orderly offering of prayer and praise to Almighty God. In stronger language than was ordinarily his practice, the Bishop of Dunblane ordered that ". . . the reciting of the ten commandments, and the belief, according to the acts of former Synods, is no Lord's day to be omitted; nor is this only or mainly meant as a help to the peoples learning the words of them, and so being able to repeat them, but as a solemn publication of the law of God, as the rule of our life, and a solemn profession of our believing the articles of our Christian faith, and for the quickening of our affections towards both".[3]

Instructions were also issued concerning church manners. The Synod of Aberdeen "recommended . . . that, in tyme of publick prayer, people sall pray either standing or kneeling, as the most reverend gesture in prayer". The ministers were also warned to "be exemplarie therein themselves, and that at the singing of the doxologie the people sall stand and not sit".[4] Leighton warned

[1] *Alford*, pp. 360–61.   [2] Scougall, *Works*, p. 329.
[3] Leighton, *Works*, II, 437. See also pp. 433–44.   [4] *Alford*, p. 5.

against "their most indecent sitting at prayer", and urged his people "to kneel or stand, as conveniently they may, that we may worship, both with our bodies and with our souls, Him that made both . . . Oh! how needful is that invitation to be rung in our ears, that seem wholly to have forgot it, 'Oh! come, and let us worship, and bow down and kneel before the Lord our Maker'." [1] However, church customs are not easily altered, and in 1678 the Presbytery of Alford complained that in public prayer the people sat and kept their heads covered, "making no more difference in their behaviour in the house of God than in their privat houses, or rather less, seeing that they kneeled in their privat worship . . .". [2]

The pulpit continued to occupy a place of first importance in the Restoration church. Indeed, it fulfilled many of the functions of a modern newspaper. Here proclamations from Parliament or the Privy Council were read, notices of fast-days or days of thanksgiving were made public, and sinners were rebuked. The delivery of sermons was one of the minister's chief duties. Ordinarily he was expected to preach three times every week—during the two Sunday services and at one weekday service. In 1674 it was reported of Mr Patrick Chalmer, minister of Inverboyndie, that "great pains [were] taken by the minister in preaching on the Sabbath and lectureing on the Tuesday". [3] The Minister of Glenbucket was accused by the Presbytery of Alford of not preaching in the afternoon, but he excused himself on the ground that he was prevented by "the falling down of the uvula of his craig [throat] occasioned by his preaching in the forenoon, but that in place thereof he frequently catechized". The excuse was accepted. [4] It was especially difficult to maintain the weekday sermon, and sometimes it was abandoned. In 1686 the Minister of Banff reported "that he having broke off from weeklie sermons becaus people did not attend and some desiring them again he was resolved to begin on Tuesday next, but if he had not the face of a congregation he would give them up again". [5]

[1] *Works*, II, 438–9.   [2] *Alford*, p. 293.   [3] *Banff*, II, 42.
[4] *Alford*, p. xxxii.   [5] *Banff*, II, 57.

The usual custom was to preach from an ordinary—that is, one book was selected from which sermons were preached over a period of weeks or even months, the preacher working his way through the book, one text at a time. The Synod of Aberdeen (1664) ordered "that evrie Lord's day the text wherupon the minister preaches, and how often he preaches, and dyets of catechising, be insert in the severall Sessione books . . .".[1] Thus we find in the kirk-session minutes of Banff:

> November 22 [1663]—The minister continued in his ordinary, beginning with John, ch. xvii., for the forenoon, afternoon being Matt., ch. vi., beginning with the Lord's Prayer.[2]

Sermons could not be read, but had to be delivered from memory. This was a difficult assignment, and the preparation of three weekly sermons, plus the occasional exercising and adding which were done at presbytery, was a major duty for every minister. Gilbert Burnet wrote of his own preparation:

> I read the Scripture with great application and got a great deal of it by heart, and accustomed myself as I was riding or walking to repeat parcells of it. I went through the Bible to consider all the texts proper to be preached on, and studied to understand the literal meaning of the words. . . . I accustomed myself on all occasions to form my meditations into discourse, and spoke aloud what occurred to my thoughts. I went over the body of Divinity frequently . . . and formed a way of explaining every part of it in the easiest and clearest way I could, and I spent a great part of every day in talking over to myself my thoughts of these matters. But that which helped me most was that I studied to live in frequent recollection, observing myself, and the chain of thoughts that followed all good or bad inclinations, and thus by a course of meditation and prayer I arrived at a great readiness in preaching that has continued ever with me from that time.[3]

The length of sermons is an eloquent testimony to the patience of the hearers. Nicoll reports that at the Parliament of 1662, when bishops were to be restored, "thair wes ane sermound taght by

---

[1] *Alford*, p. 59.   [2] *Banff*, ii, 43.
[3] Clarke and Foxcroft, *Life of Burnet*, pp. 57–8.

Mr George Halyburtoun minister at Peerth, now Bischop of Dunkell, quhilk indured the space of 2 houres and moir".[1] This was longer than usual. Dr Henderson has analysed a number of seventeenth-century sermons and concluded "that the normal length of a sermon was about an hour".[2]

Sermons of the period usually followed the outline of "doctrines, reasons, and uses".[3] Gilbert Burnet was not the only one to criticize the preaching of the Restoration Church:

> What are preachings turned to? long formal discourses, often impertinent and unintelligible to the vulgar, at best wrought out wt an operose method and stuffed wt pedantry . . . how dry are our long preachments, where the poor people must be worried an hour at least at such mean stuff.[4]

Robert Leighton in his "Charges to the Clergy" showed his interest in improving the quality of preaching:

> If the minister think fit to make his sermon for the time upon some part of what, by himself, or by his appointment, hath been read, it may do well; and possibly so much the better, the longer the text be, and the shorter the sermon be; for, it is greatly to be suspected, that our usual way of very short texts, and very long sermons, is apt to weary people more, and profit them less.[5]

Leighton's own sermons, though not typical of the spirit of the times, were among the finest written during the period. Burnet says that "His preaching had a sublimity both of thought and expression in it; and, above all, the grace and gravity of his pronunciation was such that few heard him without a very sensible emotion. . . . His style was rather too fine: but there was a majesty and beauty in it that left so deep an impress, that I cannot yet forget the sermons I heard him preach thirty year[s] ago." [6]

In a sermon on "Divine Grace and Holy Obedience", Leighton wrote:

> Few, few are acquainted with that delightful contemplation of God, that ventilates and raises this flame of love. Petty things bind

---

[1] Nicoll, p. 366.   [2] Henderson, op. cit., p. 195.   [3] Ibid., p. 204.
[4] *Miscellany of the Scottish History Society*, II, 353.
[5] *Works*, II, 438.   [6] *History*, I, 241.

and contract our spirits, so that they feel little joy in God, little ardent active desire to do him service, to crucify sin, to break and undo self-love with us, to root up our own wills to make room for his. . . . One glance of God, a touch of his love will free and enlarge the heart, so that it can deny all, and part with all, and make an entire renouncing of all, to follow Him.[1]

After the sermon and some final prayers, the service ended with a blessing. The Synod of Aberdeen ordered (1662) that "the Readers of the Scriptures on the Lord's day shall not pronounce the blessing over the people, but shall leave that to be done by the minister, but the Reader on the week day may pronounce the blessing, as also he may pronounce it on the Lord's day if the minister shall be . . . absent . . .".[2]

Each parish was expected to have an annual celebration of the Eucharist. In 1685 the Synod of St Andrews required ministers to "celebrate the sacrament of our Lord's Supper twyce everie yeare, att least once, under the paine of being suspended".[3] In Aberdeen "the Lord Bishop . . . thought fitt to recommend to the brethren to be carefull in administering the Sacrament of the Lord's Supper at Easter yeirly . . .".[4] The same injunction had been issued by the Bishop and Synod of Moray in 1677 which required "that each broyr thrise every yeir preach against rebellion . . . and that the sacrament be celebrat at Easter".[5]

The records of the period indicate the way in which this duty was fulfilled. Mr Duncan MacCulloch was Minister of Glen Urqhart from 1647 until 1671. During the entire time the sacrament was not celebrated.[6] On 1 October 1679 the moderator of the Presbytery of Inverness "enquyred iff the Bretheren . . . have celebrat the Sacrament of the Lords Supper since the last Synod, and it is found yt most of the Bretheren hawe not given it, and ther reason was yt the frequent charges yt ther people gott to be in armes against the McDonalds obstructed ther friedom to that great work".[7] An episcopal visitation to the Church of Foderty

<hr />

[1] *Works*, III, 292.   [2] *Alford*, pp. 1–2.
[3] *Dunkeld*, II, 69.   [4] *Alford*, p. 369.
[5] *Inverness and Dingwall*, p. 84.
[6] Ibid., p. xxi.   [7] Ibid., p. 95.

by the Bishop of Ross in 1665 revealed "that the sacrament was not given in the said Parish thes twelve yeers bygone".[1] A visitation at Weem by the Presbytery of Dunkeld in 1682 discovered that the minister, who was admitted to the charge in 1664, had never celebrated the Sacrament.[2]

In spite of this record, the ideal of an annual celebration was clearly stated and reasonably approached by many. In 1671 the minutes of the Presbytery of Alford record the fact that "Mr. Adam Barclay, Mr. Thomas Garden, Mr. William Christie, and Mr. Robert Irving, and the moderator declared that they did celebrate the sacrament on Easter and Mr. George Watsone, and Mr. Walter Ritchie Ap: 16".[3] Five years later five ministers of the same presbytery reported "that they had celebrat the Sacrament of the Lord's Supper on Easter, as also the ministers of Alford and Auchindore reported that they had celebrat the Holy Eucharist on Pentecost".[4] In 1668 the Chronicler of Fraser wrote "it was a pleasure to see that famely come to church, especially at a sacrament time. The last Easter the Holy Eucharist was solemnly celebrated at Mons Mariae! . . . Lord, make thy seales and sacraments effectuall for that great end thow hast appointed them for. . . ."[5]

Another alteration which took place at the Restoration was the provision for private communion, at least in some areas. In 1662 the Synod of Aberdeen ordered that "privat communione be not denied by any minister", and should there be a "plague of pestilence, then . . . the minister is free to give it to the diseased persones . . .".[6]

Celebrations were preceded by a preparation service and followed by a service of thanksgiving. Sometimes the sacrament would be held on two successive Sundays to accommodate the large crowds and to give everyone an opportunity to attend. A typical schedule was that of Elgin in 1684. On 17 May a preparation service was held; the sacrament was celebrated the following

[1] *Inverness and Dingwall*, p. 312. [2] *Dunkeld*, 1, 440.
[3] *Alford*, p. 170. [4] Ibid., p. 218.
[5] *Chronicles of the Frasers*, p. 474. [6] *Alford*, p. 2.

day, and on 19 May a thanksgiving sermon was preached. The
same procedure was followed the next week on 24, 25 and 26 May.[1]

The preparation service was itself the climax of a long period
of preparation, usually called catechizing or examining. *The
Register of the Kirk-Session of Rattray* illustrated the usual procedure:

> Apprill 10, 1670.—Quhilk day, intimatione was made of examina-
> tione of the severall quarters, in order to the celebratione of the
> Sacrament, as they wer formerlie appointed, and exorted to kip ther
> dyets.
> The 10th July 1670—Quhilk day, the people in their quarters
> being catichized, the celebratione of the Lord's supper is appointed
> to be this day eight dayes . . .[2]

At the end of this long process of preparation, which in the case
of Rattray lasted for three months, tickets were issued to those
who had been adequately prepared. These were collected by the
elders and deacons at the time of the celebration. At first made
of paper, the tickets were later made of leather or metal.[3] This
process of careful preparation and the use of tickets for admission
were based on a doctrine of "fencing the table". The dangers of
unworthy communion and the desire to protect the sacrament
from profanation were the motivation for a long process of
preparation, examination, and exclusion of the unprepared.

Attendance at catechism as well as at the celebration was
required. The Kirk-Session of Elgin "being informed that many
wilfullie absented themselves both from the Sacrament of the
Lords Supper and also from the catechising frequentlie therfor
. . . have ordained all such to be censured be publick rebuik
before the congregatione for the first time".[4]

The whole process of preparation, celebration and thanksgiving
is illustrated in the Register of the Kirk-Session of Rattray:

> The 2d of Agust, 1668.—The minister preached Luke 22, verse 1:
> afternoon Luk 22. 1. Quhilk day, the celebratione of the Sacrament

---

[1] *Elgin*, II, 314.   [2] *Dunkeld*, II, 74.
[3] "The celebration of Communion in Scotland since the Reformation",
in *Records of the Scottish Church History Society*, IV, 48 ff.
[4] *Elgin*, II, 300–301.

was intimat againe to be that day eight dayes, and on Thursday such
as wanted tickets to come and receive them, and on Saturnday the
preparatione sermon to be, to quhich they wer exhorted to be
present be ten hours.

On Saturday, Agust 8th, being the day of preparatione of the
Lord's Supper, Mr. John Fyffe, minister at Ruthven, preached.
. . . After sermon, the minister exhorted the congregatione to
mynd seriouslie quhat ane actione they wer to goe about, debarring
all ignorants, scandalous persons, and persons at variance, strangers
from other congregationes without testimonialls. The dyett of meit-
ting to-morrow to be at eight a cloak in the morning. Also their was
deacons and elders appointit to the severall doores for the contributione, and for right ordering of the elements and raising and filling
the tables.

The 9th Agust, 1668.—Being the day of the celebratione of the
Sacrament of the Lord's Supper, after reiding of the Word, the
minister preached; . . . after sermon, debarring all ignorant persones and persons at variance, went to the tables, and, according to
the words of institutione, did consecrat the elements by prayer, and
served the tables. After all, the action was closed with exhortatione
and prayer.

In the afternoon, ane Thanksgiving sermon was preached by Mr.
Thomas Blair, minister at Blair. . . . After sermon the people wer
exhorted to convein the morrow be ten houres for heiring another
sermon of Thanksgiving. [On Monday, a sermon was preached by
the minister of Cargill.] [1]

Several characteristic features of the Communion Service can
be seen in this account. Three ministers from nearby churches
came to assist with the long and taxing service. Several tables,
usually covered with tablecloths, were set up in the body of the
church. The communicants sat at the tables and were served the
bread and wine there. The wine was customarily distributed in a
common cup.

The records also show the "utensils" which a well-equipped
parish was expected to have. The Church of Keig reported (1685)
that "they were provyded of two tiun cups for the Communion,
a laver [for baptism] and a bason, two table cloathes, and a Kirk
Bible",[2] while at Clatt (1680) "there were two tables and a

[1] *Dunkeld*, II, 78.   [2] *Alford*, p. 364.

linnen cloath for covering for the same, two silver cups for the use of the holy Communion".[1] An account of the Restoration practice written in 1690 described the procedure in Edinburgh:

> Each of these Churches has its own Utensils, Basons, Lavers, Chargers, Chalices, Communion Table-Cloths, &c. all Dedicated long ago by private Persons, who lived in the respective Parishes. A Church Treasurer is chosen yearly by the Church-Sessions, to whom these Utensils are concredited, and to these Sessions he is accountable for them at the Years-end.[2]

Such complete equipment was not true of all parishes. At Kirk-hill in the Presbytery of Inverness, the minister reported (1682) that "he had a very good large table, two good towells, a Basin also, but yt he borrowed silver cups yearely", while the Minister of Petty "declared that he had a Table onely, other things he borrowed".[4] The Church of Daviot was completely destitute, and had none of the "necessaries for the celebraon of the Lords Supper".[5]

Daily prayers were held each morning and evening in many of the larger churches. In the diocese of Aberdeen, fifteen churches were required to have regular daily services in 1662.[6] In that same year Leighton urged his clergy to have "daily public prayer, in churches, morning and evening, with reading of the Scriptures . . . and the people exhorted to frequent them".[7] Apparently the response to this plan was so poor that he never urged it again, and its absence is conspicuous in his later charges. In fact, there seems to be no evidence that daily services were either prevalent or well attended.

One of the duties of a minister was to catechize the faithful. Ideally this was to be done regularly throughout the year, but catechizing only as a preparation for Communion was more common. The effectiveness of the discipline was greatly limited by the lack of any official catechism. Leighton constantly urged

---

[1] *Alford*, p. 316.
[2] *An Account of the Present Persecution*, p. 52.
[3] *Inverness and Dingwall*, p. 109.
[4] Ibid., p. 110. [5] Ibid., p. 106.
[6] *Alford*, p. 1. *Works*, II, 434.

his clergy to use a more "short and plain form of catechism",[1] and in 1667 he made a further proposal:

It seems absolutely necessary that each minister would resolve on some short and plain form of catechism, for the use of his people; for, it is not, I think, to be imagined, that ever people, will have any fixed knowledge of the articles of religion, by lax, and continually varied, discourses and forms, or by catechisms too long and too hard for them; and would some draw up several short forms, they might be revised at the next Synod, and possibly one framed out of them, which, by consent, might be appointed for the use of this diocese for the interim, till one shall be published for the whole church.[2]

As far as can be discovered, no catechism was ever issued. In 1683 the Synod of Aberdeen also ordered the preparation of "ane Catechisme drawn up in the best and plainest manner, touching all the principall heads of Christianitie, which are most necessarie to be known by all".[3] However, by 1687 the catechism had not yet been prepared,[4] and there is no indication that it was ever issued.

Leighton himself wrote a catechism which shows the marks of his own deep piety.

Q. What is the final portion of them that truly repent and believe, and obey the gospel?
A. The blessed life of angels, in the vision of God forever.[5]

There are a surprising number of references to the Church year in Restoration literature. In 1665 there was a good harvest, "qhilk was the cause that a number of fee'd servants . . . did marry at Martinmas".[6] In 1674 Cuningham noted in his diary: "I compleited the first year's boarding to the Lady betwixt Whitsunday 1673 and Whits: 1674."[7]

These terms may be the result of a social conservatism which continued to use names that no longer had religious significance. However, this is not true in every case. The *Chronicles of the*

[1] *Works*, II, 445.
[2] Ibid., pp. 446-7.
[3] *Alford*, p. 350.
[4] Ibid., p. 379.
[5] *Works*, IV, 201.
[6] *Domestic Annals*, II, 305.
[7] *Cunningham's Diary*, p. 2.

Frasers (1672) record that "my Lord Lovat at his return home to Beuly ordered preparations to be made for the feast of Epiphany, called Uphallyday, to be kept at his owne house, January 6".[1] In 1663 "The Ascentioune day, falling this yeir upone the 29 day of Maij, wes keipit in Edinburgh and mony uther pairtes of this kingdome".[2] "Upon the 5 day of November, being Monday, 1666, the solempnitie for the Gun powder treasone was keiped at Edinburgh by preaching, ringing of bellis, setting on of bonfyres, and schooting of canons." [3] In 1662 "the threttie day of November this yeir fallin upone ane Saboth day, and being a day callit Sant Androis day, many of our nobles, barones, gentrie, and utheris of this kingdome, pat on that day ane liveray . . . for reverence thairof. This being a novaltie, I thoght guid to record, becaus it wes nevir in use heirtofoir since the Reformatioun." [4]

In 1662 the Privy Council forbade the eating of flesh meat on the "weekly fish days, viz. Wednesday, Friday, Saturday [as well as] the time of Lent".[5] This had been abandoned in 1640, but Wodrow was glad to see it revived "for the preservation of the young bestial and the consumption of our fish, which the Lord hath so bountifully given us".[6] In 1666 "upone the first day of Januarij . . . ther was als mutch drinking and carrussing as in formar tymes".[7]

Most of these are isolated cases of Feasts which were celebrated irregularly or only in some areas. However, two Feasts of major importance were revived at the Restoration: 29 May and Christmas Day.

By Act of Parliament, 29 May was to be celebrated throughout the kingdom in honour of both the birth of Charles II and his Restoration. It was widely observed and the record of that fact carefully noted. In 1674 the members of the Presbytery of Fordyce "reported that they had observed the twentie-nynt day off May according to the ordinance of the Lo/Bishop and Synod", and

---

[1] *Chronicles of the Frasers*, p. 501.   [2] Nicoll, p. 391.
[3] Ibid., p. 451.   [4] Ibid., p. 384.
[5] Wodrow, *History*, I, 318–19.
[6] Stephen's summary of Wodrow's argument, *History*, II, 508–9.
[7] Nicoll, p. 445.

similar references occur in all records.[1] In 1664, 29 May occurred on Whitsunday, which was regarded as a most auspicious omen.[2] Those with covenanting sympathies looked on the celebration with considerable suspicion. Brodie wrote in his diary: "29.—This is the anniversari of the King's Return; and albeit a civil remembranc of it, and with thankfulnes, be lawful, yet the day is noe way differing from other days." [3]

References to Christmas occur frequently in the records. In 1668 the Presbytery of Dingwall received "a letter sent from the Bishop [of Ross] ordaining the Brethren to preach an Christs nativitie day".[4] By 1678 "All the brethren had preached on 25th December except Mr. George Cumine who wes tender for the tyme".[5] In 1684 "the Moderator recomends to the Bren to observe the feast of our Saviours nativitie", and in January all report that they did.[6] Sometimes the feast was called by another name. The *Chronicles of the Frasers* record . . . "it being Yewell Royall falling upon Sunday, most of the gentlemen being at sermon convoyed my Lord from church home . . . [then a] solem, handsom, opulent Christmas feast".[7] In Edinburgh it was customary for the Town Council to order all businesses to close for the day.[8]

Part of the duty of a minister was the administration of the occasional services of baptism, marriage, and burial. Parents were expected to have their children baptized at an early age, and the Presbytery of Dingwall disciplined "Mr. Johne McKillican [who] . . . had not required baptism to his child, twentie days and more being expired".[9] While there were no formal godparents, we do find such entries as "August 28, 1663—Foyla Groat (father); Mary (child), Hugh Groat, William Morison, witnesses".[10] Witnesses were always men. In 1663 the Session of Elgin ordered that "the sacrament of baptisme is to be administered only upon

---

[1] *Banff*, II, 42. For other examples, see *Inverness and Dingwall*, pp. 315, 357.
[2] Nicoll, p. 413. For a description of the celebration in 1663, see p. 391.
[3] *Diary of the Lairds of Brodie*, p. 299.
[4] *Inverness and Dingwall*, p. 321.   [5] Ibid., p. 325.
[6] Ibid., p. 356.   [7] *Chronicles of the Frasers*, p. 472.
[8] Nicoll, pp. 385, 453.   [9] *Inverness and Dingwall*, p. 313.
[10] *Parish Records of Canisbay*, Scottish Record Society Publications, December 1914, p. 13.

Sunday and Tysday and not to come to the minister on other day except there be necessitie".[1]

At the baptism there was a sermon, questions put to the father, the Creed, prayers, and "then with Water out of a Bason conveniently fasten'd to the Pulpit-side, the Minister sprinkled the Child in the Name of Father, Son and Holy Ghost".[2] The congregation was dismissed with prayers and a blessing.

A marriage contract or "engagement" was agreed upon by the prospective husband and wife. Each party had a "cautioner" who guaranteed that a fine would be paid to the kirk (usually 10*l. scots*) if the contract were broken.[3]

After the engagement, banns were announced on three successive Sundays from the pulpit. In 1682 the Synod of Aberdeen cautioned the clergy that "no persons be married without licence from the Bishop, except they be three severall Lord's days publicklie claimed befor the congregation, and that none be proclaimed thrice in one day".[4]

At the marriage there was a sermon, and questions were asked of the couple. They joined "hands, without using the Ring, and thereupon [the minister] pronounces 'em Man and Wife'".[5] They were then dismissed with a blessing. Wedding parties, called "penny brydalls" from the custom of requiring each guest to bring a penny to pay the fiddler, were common, and resulted in regulative legislation by the kirk. In 1675 the Sub-Synod of Moray issued a long resolution which limited the number of persons to sixteen and forbade "all piping, fidling and dancing wthout doores . . . [and] all obscene lascivious and Promiscuous dancing within doores".[6]

---

[1] *Elgin*, II, 302.   [2] Morer, *Short Account*, p. 63.
[3] The full procedure is preserved in the Marriage Register of Canisbay. In 1653 "George Sinclar in ye parishe of Dunett was matrimoniallie contracted with Christiane Ghom in ye parishe of Cannesbey. The said George fand John Bowman in Dunatt; and Christane, Thomas Sandisone, cautioners for their mutuall performa'cie, according to ye order under ye paid of 10 punds scotts, in case of failze in any of ye said parties to be paid to the Kirks use." *Parish Records of Canisbey*, pp. 15, 17.
[4] *Alford*, p. 336.   [5] Morer, *Short Account*, p. 65.
[6] *Inverness and Dingwall*, p. 121.

Applications for divorce or annulment were received by the Church. In 1670 the Presbytery of Inverness received an application from Elspit Nickphaile, who had been married for nine years, during which time her husband, John Taylor, "neiyr adhered to her nor performed any duty belonging to a husband in any case quatsoever, especially in ye wedlock bond, he being *frigidej it impotentis naturij*, as was well known". The case was referred to the synod, which granted a decree of nullity.[1] In 1666 the Bishop of Ross received a petition from Donald Kempe

> supplicating the said Reverent father . . . that wheras his wife Jonet Vrgrt had fallen in that heinous sin of adulterie with one Johne Kaird a vagrant, and had brought furth a child to him; That the said Reverend Father would be pleased either to speak the Commissrs of Rosse, or els to write to the Commssrs of Edr. for a divorce from the said Janet.[2]

The request was granted.

Burial services were abolished by the General Assembly of 1638,[3] but the old practice was revived during the time of episcopacy. At the funeral of Andrew Fairfowl, Archbishop of Glasgow (1663),

> . . . his corps wer laid doun upon a buird just befoir the pulpit, coverit with murning. The toun bell rang for convening the pepill to his funerall sermound just at four in the eftirnoon; quhair, numberis of pepill being convenit, rather to behold the ceremony then the preacher, thair was ane sermond . . . [then] the corps wer laid in the bottome of a kitche [cart], coverit above with murning, and careyed with two horses, all cled in murning apperell, wer transportit from the New Kirk of Edinburgh to the Abay church of Halyrudhous, four trumpettis sounding.[4]

The following year, the sermon preached at the funeral of the Earl of Leven was "the first funeral-sermon that hath been preached in Fife these twenty-four years last past, or more".[5]

Not all those who departed this life were honoured with a

---

[1] *Inverness and Dingwall*, pp. 6–8.   [2] Ibid., pp. 316–17.
[3] Rogers, *Social History of Scotland*, I, 153.
[4] Nicoll, pp. 403–4.   [5] *Domestic Annals*, II, 299.

sermon, and in 1684 the Presbytery of Inverness requested advice on a special situation:

> . . . they were severals times importuned to preach funerall sermonds when persons were buried who hade left no monument of their charitie to the poor, or oyr necessarie works, notwithstanding of theri ability, Therefor they desired . . . whether or no such persons should haue the honour of a funerall sermon.[1]

According to Morer, the usual practice was only a procession to the grave, "the Coffin being covered with a large Black Cloth or Velvet Pall, sprinkled with Herbs and Flowers. . . . Being arrived at the Grave, they put in the dead Corps with little ceremony, and then the Company immediately return home."[2]

Fast-days were proclaimed for various causes. On 3 May 1665 a "publick General Fast . . . for the blessing of Almightie God . . . in the war against the United Provines"[3] was ordered by the King and widely observed throughout the kingdom. On 2 March 1665 the Kirk-Session of Banff ordered "Ane fast . . . to be the next Sabboth that the Lord wold turn away the foulnes of the weather".[4] Fasts were ordered for the plague in England,[5] because of poor crops,[6] or to celebrate a naval victory.[7] In many areas the Sunday prior to a celebration of the Lord's Supper was a fast-day.[8] On a fast-day all citizens were

> . . . to cease from all the works of their ordinary callings, and to repair to their respectiv paroch churches, and there make solemn confession of their sins . . . praying, mourning, fasting, and . . . other devotions.[9]

In the Highland parishes Gaelic (called Irish in the seventeenth century) was spoken by most of the people, and the Church constantly faced the problem of finding ministers who could speak that language. There were ten Highland parishes in the Presbytery of Dunkeld; in three of them the minister could

[1] *Inverness and Dingwall*, p. 118.
[2] Morer, *Short Account*, pp. 66–8.
[3] *Dunkeld*, I, 404.
[4] *Banff*, II, 46.
[5] *Inverness and Dingwall*, p. 313.
[6] *Alford*, p. 204.
[7] *Banff*, II, 46.
[8] For example, ibid., p. 47.
[9] *Dunkeld*, I, 412.

speak only English.[1] A visitation at Weem (1682) discovered that
the minister had never celebrated the Lord's Supper, partly
"because of his ignorance in the Irish language. . . . As to
catechizing, he told he did his endeavour to informe himself in
the Irish toung that he might catechize those lying at a distance".[2]
Gaelic-speaking ministers customarily preached one sermon in
English and the other in Gaelic. In 1671 the elders and gentlemen
of Doores declared of their minister "that they were refreshed
very much by him Sabbathly both in english and irish language
. . .".[3]

The Restoration Church also has the distinction of having
produced a Psalter and later a Bible in Gaelic. On 11 December
1673 Mr Robert Kirk, Minister of Aberfoyle, "petitioned the
Privy Council for liberty to print a translation, executed by himself, of the last hundred of the Psalms into the Irish tongue". He
also supervised the printing of a Gaelic Bible in London in 1685.[4]

At the door of every church there was a "kirk bred" or "brod"
or "box", which was a large chest designed to receive contributions for the poor. The chest had two locks, the respective keys of
which were in possession of different members of the session.[5]
From this fund, alms were distributed by the minister and elders.
In addition, at every celebration of the Lord's Supper a special
collection was taken for the poor. In 1673 the following collection
and distribution of alms took place at Banff:

April 13—Sacrament, collected at the doors, 6 l. 14s. 6d.; at the
tables, 11 l. 7s. 10d.
April 14—Thanksgiving sermon. Distributed poor's money: May 5,
12 l. 2s. 4d.; August 5, 12 l. 4d.; November 2, 13 l. 0s. 4d.; February 2, 13 l. 12s. Ten are Seatown poor and seventeen are town
poor.[6]

In 1687 the Kirk-Session of Aberdeen found that many wander-
ing beggars were seeking funds, and ordered "that all the poor
within the parish . . . conveen on Sunday . . . at the church

[1] *Dunkeld*, II, 101 ff.   [2] Ibid., I, 441.
[3] *Inverness and Dingwall*, p. 9.   [4] *Domestic Annals*, II, 361.
[5] *Cunningham's Diary*, p. xx.   [6] *Banff*, II, 49.

that after inspection taken ther may be an exact list of those that
are esteemed trulie indigent and poor who are to have tokens
given them for distinguishing them from Stranger beggers".[1]

Often authorized by the Privy Council or a bishop, collections
in all churches were also taken for special emergencies. In 1684
a general collection was held for the 306 families of Kelso whose
homes and goods were destroyed by fire, the people themselves
barely escaping from "the flames and rage of the smoak".[2] The
Synod of Ross authorized a collection for "the distrest men of
Portpatrick, some wherof were captives with the Turks, and others
of them ruined in fortune",[3] and a decade later a collection
was taken for "ane Mecurius Lascaris, a minister of the Greek
Church".[4]

The parish churches also collected funds for public projects,
such as harbours, bridges, and piers. A nineteenth-century com-
mentator wrote: "None were more active in the work of building
bridges than the Scottish clergy . . . most of the old Scottish
bridges were paid for with moneys collected in great measure by
them".[5] In the Presbytery of Dunkeld a collection was taken in
1663 "for repairing the harbour of Kelburn and the bridge of
Almond"; in the next year for "the bridge of Dee"; and in 1666
for "repairing the harbour of Inverkeithing".[6] In 1683 the
Presbytery of Dunkeld received a request from Arthur Ssoiles in
Bostell, "supplicating the Presbyterie for a contributione to the
repairing of the bruse [brew-house] of Alnes. The usefulness of the
work considderd, the Bren promise sexteen pounds scotts." [7]

The ideal of a school in every parish was upheld by the *First
Book of Discipline*, but the establishment of such a thoroughgoing
educational system was the work of several generations. The Act
of the Privy Council in 1616 and the Act of Parliament in 1633
ratifying the "act of counsall anent Plantatione of Schooles" were
the legal bases for schools during the Restoration. The Act of 1616

[1] *Records of Old Aberdeen*, ii, 87.   [2] *Dunkeld*, i, 409.
[3] *Inverness and Dingwall*, p. 308.   [4] *Alford*, p. 303.
[5] *Cunningham's Diary*, p. xviii.   [6] *Dunkeld*, i, 420–21.
[7] *Inverness and Dingwall*, p. 349.

required "that a scoole salbe establisheit, and a fitt persone appointit to teache the same, upoun the expensis of the parrochinnairs . . . in everie parroche of this kingdome",[1] and this was somewhat strengthened by the Act of 1633. In 1665 the Synod of St Andrews ordered "that the brethren walk according to the Act of Parliament in King James' tyme for the setling of scools in their several parishes".[2]

Visitation records reveal something of the condition of kirk-schools. At the visitation of Inverness, the minister and elders declared "they were well satisfied with the thriveing theirof . . . and well pleased with yr schoolmaster".[3] In 1663 Commissioners who were appointed to visit the School of Alford reported that they "hade found the master diligently discharging his duty, and the scholars profiting".[4] When Gilbert Burnet became Minister of Saltoun in 1665, he discovered that there was a schoolmaster but no school building. Through his efforts, a small building was erected.[5]

However, in many parishes no school existed. No doubt the heritors were often not wealthy, and excuses were only too frequent. The elders of Moy reported that "there was not a school in the Pariochin partlie because the townes within the pariochin were far distant one from the other".[6] The elders of Daviot reported that they had a school "but that the Schoolmster was forced to leave them for want of mantenance".[7] Of the sixteen parishes in the Exercise of Alford, seven had schools.[8]

Salaries for schoolmasters were especially low. The Act of 1646 ordered a minimum salary of 100 marks (5l. 5s. sterling) and a maximum of 200 marks (10l. 10s. sterling). Although the Act was repealed, these amounts continued to be representative during the Restoration. The schoolmaster also usually served as parish clerk and would augment his stipend by fees received from baptisms, marriages, and burials (or mort-cloth fees).

[1] Source Book of Scottish History, III, 402. [2] Dunkeld, II, 89.
[3] Inverness and Dingwall, p. 23. [4] Alford, p. 15.
[5] Clarke and Foxcroft, Life of Burnet, p. 60.
[6] Inverness and Dingwall, p. 18.
[7] Ibid., p. 20. [8] Alford, p. xliii.

Knowledge of the classics, and especially of Latin, was a major qualification for schoolmasters. The Exercise of Alford appointed "Mr. Arthur Forbes . . . to handle the Prologue of Perseus in a grammaticall and prosodicall way, in order to his admission to be Schoolmaster at Keig".[1] "Mr. Alexr Ross, . . . was admitted schoolmaster at Invernes . . . and for his tryalls hade the third ode of Horace and hade his oratione *de vanitate hum. scientiae*, and all oyr tryalls usuall in the like case, and was fullie approven. . . ."[2]

The struggle to establish schools in every parish was a long one, but their number and quality continued to increase, so that by 1758 the Society in Scotland for Propagating Christian Knowledge reported that four-fifths of the parishes had schools.[3]

The influence of the Church upon the daily lives of parishioners was immense. The long Sunday services, the administration of the charitable and educational institutions of the land, and the constant activity of the Church courts were ways in which the dominant position of the Church was maintained.

The re-establishment of episcopacy had less effect upon parish life than upon any other aspect of the Church of Scotland. Apart from the fact that laymen were no longer entitled to attend the meetings of presbytery and higher Church courts, no alteration of importance took place. The changes in worship were minor in character and, in any case, were the restoration of traditional elements and not the introduction of anything new. Parish churches in Scotland knew nothing of the kind of upheaval which parishes in England experienced during the middle of the century. Throughout the whole of the seventeenth century the basic structure and pattern of parish life was unchanged, and the reintroduction of episcopacy in 1662 did nothing to alter that continuity.

---

[1] *Alford*, p. 267.   [2] *Inverness and Dingwall*, p. 42.   [3] *Dunkeld*, II, 91.

7

MOVEMENTS OF THOUGHT AND RELATIONS WITH THE CHURCH OF ENGLAND

THE Westminster Confession of Faith had been ratified by Parliament in 1649,[1] but it was abolished by the Act Rescissory of 1661. This latter action automatically restored the older Scots Confession, which had been approved by Parliament in 1560, and again in 1567,[2] as the official statement of faith. Subscription to the Confession of 1560 was required by the Test Act of 1681. The Confession was largely the work of John Knox and was a more moderate statement of Calvinism than that produced by the Westminster divines.

However, the Westminster Confession does not seem to have disappeared completely, and there is some evidence that it continued to be of influence along with the more official Confession of 1560. Burnet wrote:

Dalrymple proposed [for the Test Act] the confession of faith agreed on . . . in parliament in 1567, which was the only confession that had then the sanction of a law. That was a book so worn out of use, that scarce any in the whole parliament had ever read it. None of the bishops had, as appeared afterwards; for these last 30 years the only confession of faith that was read in Scotland was that which the assembly of divines at Westminster had set out, . . . and the bishops had left it in possession, though the authority that enacted it was annulled.[3]

A defender of the Restoration Church who wrote in 1690 also mentioned both confessions:

Any moderate man will certainly think the difference between our Scots Episcopacy and Presbytery not worth the heat or danger of a

[1] Cooper, *Confessions of Faith*, p. 38. [2] Ibid., p. 29. [3] *History*, II, 314.

dispute, for first as to the doctrine, both parties are agreed, the Confession of Faith made by Mr. Knox and ratified in Parliament by King James VI and revived again in the Test Act by King Charles II, this, together with the Westminster Confession (both agreed on by the General Assembly of Presbyters) are owned next to the Word of God by both parties as the standard of the doctrine of our Church.[1]

Neither Confession was referred to very frequently during the Restoration.[2] Instead, considerable emphasis was placed upon the Apostles' Creed, and its use was required at Sunday services and at baptisms.[3]

The dominant theological climate in Scotland was Calvinist. Since Calvinism had been the major formative influence in Scotland during the entire Reformation period, it is not surprising that this theological tradition should have continued as the recognized doctrinal background of the Restoration Church. Agreement on the essentials of Calvinism can almost be assumed. In 1684 Sir George Skene, Provost of Aberdeen, wrote two prayers. The first begins: "O ETERNAL, Heart-searching, Sin-Pardoning, Lord God!" while the second is similar: "O ALMIGHTY, Dreadful, Covenant-keeping Lord, who searches the heart and tryes the reines. . . ."[4] The subjects assigned for controversy to candidates undergoing their ordination trials before presbytery are also instructive. *De peccato originali, De justificatione, De satisfactione Christi, De gratia universali, De perseverantia sanctorum, De voluntate Dei, De justitia originali, De praedestinatione,* and *De universali redemptione* are typical examples.[5] In 1670 the Presbytery of Inverness examined the books which one of their students of divinity was reading. They found "Mr. James had read Calvins Instituons and Wendeline his Theological Systeme, wt Pares, and Ursius Catecheticks, and Willets Synopsis Papismi, and Sharpes

---

[1] *Case of the Present Afflicted Clergy,* Preface; quoted in Henderson, op. cit., p. 144.
[2] The magistrates of Peebles complained to the Privy Council in 1681 that they could hardly take the Test since they had neither the "act of parliament . . . nor yet the confession of faith to which it related". *Domestic Annals,* II, 429.
[3] See above, pp. 125; 126, n. 1.
[4] *Memorials of the Family of Skene of Skene,* p. 241.
[5] *Inverness and Dingwall,* p. xxviii.

Course, etc.".[1] The list would have satisfied the most thorough-going Calvinist. The Established Church was accused of many things by Nonconformists, but seldom of teaching a false faith.

However, in the North of Scotland and especially in the area of Aberdeen, another current of thought was developing which represented a considerable modification of strict Calvinism. It was not so much a new movement as a revival of that tradition represented by Bishop Patrick Forbes, John Forbes, and the other Aberdeen Doctors.[2] Unwilling to concede to the Roman Church her claims of exclusive catholicity, the Aberdeen Doctors empha-sized the importance of the visible Church, unbroken continuity of the Church with the whole of her past history, careful study of the Fathers, and the rightness of episcopacy.[3] There is a largeness of spirit and thought in these men which sought to moderate the more extreme conclusions of Calvinism. The Catholic Church of Christ, Bishop Forbes wrote, is "that company of whatsoever time, place or nation, which in communion of one and the same Spirit joined to their Head, Christ, do make up the fulness of His mystical Body".[4]

Because of their refusal to accept the Covenants, these men were deprived during the rebellion. Yet many of their pupils became bishops in the Restoration, and their thought flourished once again at Aberdeen. Men like Arthur Ross, successively bishop of Argyll, Galloway, Glasgow, and St Andrews; William Scroggie, son of the Aberdeen Doctor and Bishop of Argyll; John Paterson, Bishop of Ross; Patrick Forbes, Bishop of Caithness; George Haliburton, Bishop of Dunkeld; Robert Douglas, Bishop of Brechin and Dunblane; Alexander Rose, Bishop of Moray and Edinburgh; and William Hay, Bishop of Moray, had all studied

---

[1] *Inverness and Dingwall*, p. 4.

[2] The activities of the Aberdeen Doctors centred at King's College, Aber-deen, during the reign of Charles I. The restoration of the degree of Doctor of Divinity in 1620 gave these men their title. Those usually known as the Aberdeen Doctors were Alexander Scroggie, William Leslie James Sibbald, Robert Baron, and Alexander Ross, all of whom signed the *Replyes* and *Duplyes* to the Covenanters. Henderson, op. cit., p. 42.

[3] Snow, *Times and Life of Patrick Forbes*, ch. x.

[4] Ibid., p. 147.

under the Aberdeen Doctors. James Garden, Professor of Divinity in King's College, Aberdeen, from 1681 to 1697, had studied under Patrick Forbes. Henry Scougall held the same chair from 1674 until his early death in 1678; George Garden, Minister of Old Machar in 1679 and of the town parish of St Nicholas in 1683, became the editor of Forbes' works.

In 1663 the Bishop of Aberdeen recommended "to the haill bretherine of the Synode, that they buy . . . the queries, replyis and duplyis of the Doctoris of Aberdene, and Professors of Divinitie ther",[1] although two years later the synod was still trying to get the members to pay for the works which they had bought.[2]

In 1681 the Test Act was at first refused by many of the clergy of Aberdeen, as well as by Patrick Scougall, Bishop of Aberdeen. The Bishop's objections to the Test were not based simply on the inconsistencies and unqualified language of the oath; he also had some theological objections. The Bishop wrote:

> How can I swear that confession of faith [the Scots Confession of 1560] to be the true standard of the protestant religion and the rule of my faith . . . which in some passages is obscure and doubtful; as chap. iii, where the confession says, "that the image of God is utterly defaced in man;" and ch. xix, "the marks of the true church, the power of expounding the controverted sense of scripture and the supreme judge of controversies in the church, are dubious and disputable things." In which some things are contrary to the doctrine of this present church and all other reformed churches; as ch. xxiii, where the confession denies the ministers of the popish church to be true ministers of Christ; . . .[3]

Only after the Privy Council declared that "by the Test we do not swear to every proposition or clause [of the Confession of 1560] . . . but only to the true protestant religion, founded on the word of God, contained in that confession"[4] did most of the clergy agree to sign.

After the Revolution, when Dr Strachan of the University of

[1] *Alford*, p. 28.   [2] Ibid., p. 75.
[3] Wodrow, *History*, III, 304. Similar objections were raised by the clergy of Edinburgh. Wodrow, *History*, III, 307.   [4] Stephen, *History*, III, 226.

Edinburgh was being examined about his theology, he was not willing to place Calvin in any special position of authority. He was accused of being an Arminian. He replied:

> It has been always my Principle and practice not to espouse the particular tenets of any party, but as the ancient Philosopher said, Amicus Plato, amicus Socrates, sed magis amica veritas. So say I, Amicus Calvinus, amicus Arminius, amicus Lutherus, sed magis amica veritas, being always ready to embrace Truth by whomsoever it be maintained.[1]

About the same time, another Scotsman wrote of those who were being deprived:

> I know not so much as one amongst us, who could not live in Communion with your Church of England, and subscribe her Thirty Nine Articles. 'Tis true indeed, there be many, who are no ways inclined to be every day talking to their People of God's Decrees, and Absolute Reprobation, and Justification by Faith alone in the Presbyterian Sense, and such like Doctrines; they think their Hearers may be much more edified by Sermons, that explain the true Nature of Evangelical Faith, the Necessity of Repentance, and the Indispensibility of Gospel Obedience. . . .[2]

Nor was the reference to the Articles of the Church of England mere flattery of English readers, in as much as the possibility of adopting the Articles was considered by the Scottish bishops.[3]

All these examples are indications that a considerable modification of traditional Calvinism was taking place in some localities.

The most outstanding representative of this school of thought was Robert Leighton. It is customary to consider Leighton as within the tradition of the Aberdeen Doctors,[4] but this view can be maintained only with certain reservations. Leighton graduated from Edinburgh College, not from the University of Aberdeen. Whereas the Aberdeen Doctors opposed the Solemn League and Covenant, Leighton signed it in 1643.[5] Nor did Leighton's Accommodation Scheme find much support at Aberdeen.

---

[1] *Presbyterian Inquisition*, p. 78.
[2] *An Account of the Present Persecution*, p. 48.   [3] See above, p. 132.
[4] Snow, op. cit., pp. 169–70; Henderson, op. cit., p. 34.
[5] Butler, *Life and Letters of Leighton*, p. 195.

Yet the real difference between Leighton and the Aberdeen school was not primarily theological. Leighton's episcopate in Scotland was dominated by the pressing problem of nonconformity, and the reconciliation of the dissenters was one of the major goals of his work as a bishop. At Aberdeen nonconformity was almost non-existent, and the practical problems of the Bishop of Aberdeen were very different from those of the Archbishop of Glasgow.

The close similarity between the thought of Leighton and the Scougalls can be illustrated by a comparison of their libraries. The most striking element of the two collections is evident interest in the Cambridge Platonists, especially Henry More and John Smith, as well as in Thomas à Kempis (Leighton had three copies of the *Imitatio*). There are works by Hooker, Hammond, Andrews, Thorndyke, Jeremy Taylor, Chillingworth, and Stillingfleet; works of Calvin and other contemporary Calvinists are present, as are many of the writings of the Fathers. Dr Henderson concludes: "Each catalogue naturally contains names which are not in the other list; but there is no point of contrast between them, and the strong similarity brings out clearly the trend of this group of Scottish churchmen".[1]

It is somewhat surprising to find in Scotland, where Calvinism was so dominant, Leighton's obvious interest in the writings of Anglican divines, especially the Cambridge Platonists. Like the Cambridge Platonists, Leighton reacted strongly against the sterile controversies of his day, which he believed were destructive of true religion. Alexander Brodie was told by Leighton that "they [the bishops] placd mor relligion in ther ceremonies than in the most material things of religion; and we [the covenanters] placd more religion in opposing ther ceremonies then in the weightiest matters of the law of God".[2]

Leighton did not formally repudiate Calvinism, but he tended to ignore its distinctive theological tenets. His major interest was

---

[1] Knox, *Robert Leighton*, pp. 227–8.
[2] *Diaries of the Lairds of Brodie*, pp. 221–2. For Leighton's own statements, see above, p. 28.

in the life of Christian experience—in a vital and personal awareness of the redeeming presence of Christ. Even in his Theological
Lectures this theme recurs again and again—"Of the Happiness
of the Life to come", "Of the Christian Religion, and that it is
the true way to Happiness", "That holiness is the only way to
Happiness on this Earth", "How to regulate life, according to
the rules of religion", "Of purity of life", and "Before the
Communion".[1]

The Archbishop's *Practical Commentary on the First Epistle General
of Peter* was the most important commentary produced during
the period. "None of the other commentaries is so truly spiritual
. . . so fresh and suggestive, so interestingly illustrated, so
generous in its spirit, so free from pettiness and nearsightedness".[2]
His *Rule of Conscience* is in the tradition of English Caroline moral
theologians. Gilbert Burnet wrote of him that "I bear still the
greatest veneration for the memory of that man than I do to any
person".[3]

As was true of many of the Anglican divines, the theme of holiness dominates much of Leighton's thought. In an address to the
clergy of Dunblane he wrote:

. . . if there be within us any sparks of that divine love, you know
the best way not only to preserve them, but to excite them and blow
them up into a flame, is by the breath of prayer. Oh! prayer, the
converse of the soul with God, the breath of God in man returning to
its original. . . . All I dare say is this, I think I see the beauty of
holiness, and am enamoured with it, though I attain it not; and how
little soever I attain, would rather live and die in the pursuit of it
than in . . . all the advantages that this world affords.[4]

Thus, although Leighton made no important or original contributions to theology as such, he sought to call men away from the
controversies of the day and to turn their thought to that inner
life of holiness where there is "a shining that breaks forth and a
fount of light".[5]

[1] *Works*, vol. IV. [2] Henderson, op. cit., p. 30.
[3] *History*, I, 245. [4] *Works*, II, 452.
[5] Written by Leighton on the flyleaf of one of his copies of the Imitation.
Knox, *Robert Leighton*, p. 264.

One of the most interesting questions today concerning the Restoration Church of Scotland is the nature of her relations with the sister Church in the southern kingdom. It was not a subject considered in any systematic way during the period by members of either Church, but in the light of present-day ecumenical interest it deserves careful analysis. Clearly the Church of Scotland during the Restoration was in no sense another Anglican Church; in its ethos and its tradition of discipline and worship, the Church of the northern kingdom differed profoundly from the Church of England. Therefore it is important to state as precisely as possible the actual relationship which did exist between these two Churches, which had certain links and yet were very different.

No claim of jurisdiction over the Scottish Church was made by the Church of England. In 1661, as in 1610, the Archbishops of Canterbury and York carefully refrained from participating in the consecration of Scottish bishops so there should be no suggestion of claims to jurisdiction. In subsequent correspondence between members of the two Churches, there was no hint that the Church of England had any canonical authority over the Church of Scotland.

Both through correspondence and by visits of Scottish bishops to London, close contact between the hierarchies of the two Churches was maintained. The letters indicate the fraternal interest and sympathy which the bishops in England had for the Church of Scotland. In 1667 Archbishop Sharp wrote to Sheldon:

> You have a reserve of justice and charity for me, which I might well expect, knowing how much I had been beholdin to that paternall care I found upon all occasions from your Grace to this poor Church, and the great freindship shewn to myself, who laid open my heart to you. . . .[1]

In 1679 an encyclical letter was sent from the bishops of England to the bishops of Scotland. They wrote:

> We are extreamly glad to understand, that one of your number will shortly make us so happy as to come hither; whereby we may

---

[1] *Lauderdale Papers*, ii, Appendix, liii.

receive a more distinct account of your affairs, and know the better which way to hold out the right hand of fellowship to you, and give you the best assistance we can.[1]

In the following year the bishops acknowledged

. . . the warm concerne your Grace and the other working Prelates of England have upon all occasions manifested for our afflicted Church, and the great and seasonable help and assistance . . . received from your Lordships.[2]

In 1682 John Paterson, Bishop of Edinburgh, wrote from London to the Earl of Aberdeen:

At Lambeth were, to day, my Lords of Canterbury, London, Rochester, Lincolne, and Peterburrow. After dinner wee discoursed till 6 at night; and they were much comforted, as they professd, by the just account I gave them of the present case of our Church and State.[3]

The bishops of the Church of England thus clearly showed a warm interest in the Scottish Church, tried to learn about conditions there, and were willing to assist it wherever possible.

In a few instances the correspondence reveals something further of the nature of the relationship which existed between the two Churches. The Bishops of Scotland wrote in an encyclical letter (1680):

We think ourselves happy in being united with your Lordships in subjection to one King, and the profession of the same faith; and earnestly wish that by all other bonds and ligaments we were knit into one body.[4]

In their reply the English bishops expressed their gratitude for

. . . your daily intercessions and holy praiers for us, and that you sigh and wish (as on our part we do most earnestly) to see these two sister Churches yet more closely joyned by nearer bonds and instances of perfect union. Till that happy day shall dawn upon us. . . .[5]

---

[1] Clarke, *Collection of Letters*, p. 7.   [2] Ibid., p. 13.
[3] *Letters to the Earl of Aberdeen*, p. 44.
[4] Clarke, *Collection of Letters*, p. 8.   [5] Ibid., p. 11.

they resolve to continue letters to each other. Two months later the Scottish bishops replied that

> . . . we shall not faile, (since the happiness of a perfect union betwixt the two sister Churches in this island is, through the unhappiness and distraction of the tymes, denied us,) by frequent communicatorie letters, to improve our mutual affection and communion.[1]

Clearly the bishops did not think that the relationship which existed between the two Churches was ideal or normal. There were other "bonds and ligaments" which were necessary before they could be "knit into one body", and they could only anticipate the day when they would be "more closely joyned by nearer bonds and instances of perfect union".

Only in a few cases did the bishops indicate more specifically the nature of the barriers which they hoped to overcome. In 1685 John Paterson, Bishop of Edinburgh, wrote to Archbishop Sancroft: "The formidable rebellion being now utterlie broken in both kingdoms . . . it was verie desirable if the nationall Church could now be so happie as to have devout forms of worship setled therein. . . ."[2] Paterson was even more specific three years later in another letter to Sancroft:

> [We] can never be happie nor duelie qualified to serve the ends and securities of our holie Protestant religion, till it be brought to ane exact and regular conformitie in worship, as it is in doctrine, with the great bulwark of the Reformed religion, I meane the famous Church of England.[3]

Archbishop Ross of Glasgow did not limit the issues to matters of worship. In a letter to Sancroft (1684) he wrote:

> I wish with all my heart wee could once be happy to see heer that decency of worship, that regularity of order, and that harmonie that is in the constitutions and devotions. . . .[4]

of the Church of England.

The occasional nature of these references is disappointing but indicates again that there was no attempt in England or in Scot-

---

[1] Clarke, *Collection of Letters*, p. 14.   [2] Ibid., p. 86.
[3] Ibid., p. 92.   [4] Ibid., p. 67.

land to think out in any systematic or detailed way the nature of the relationship between the Churches of the two kingdoms. The bishops refer to their "sister Church" and recognize no point of doctrine as an issue between them. But in fact the two Churches were divided by major differences of Church order and structure as well as forms of worship. The whole Scottish disciplinary system administered by kirk-session and presbyteries had no parallel in England, and the traditional worship of the Scottish kirk was far removed from the liturgical pattern of the Book of Common Prayer. The correspondence of the bishops shows that they were well aware of these differences—though one wonders if the English bishops realized just how dissimilar the Church of Scotland was—and it was surely these issues which prevented that "perfect union" for which the bishops longed.

There is some question about the phrase "perfect union". Modern technical terminology concerning "union" and "intercommunion" was foreign to the thought of men in the seventeenth century. By "union" it is not likely that the bishops meant an administrative union which would unite the two Churches into one ecclesiastical organization. When the Scottish bishops wrote of the changes they would like to introduce into their Church, they did not suggest that they would like to make the Church of Scotland a part of the administrative structure of the English Church. They would hardly have welcomed a restoration of the jurisdiction of the Archbishop of York! The "union" which they sought seems to have been a much closer conformity of Church order, discipline, and worship than that which existed at that time. Archbishop Ross longed for the "harmony that is in the constitutions and devotions" of the Church of England.

The question of the relationship between these two Churches became a practical issue when clergy from Scotland came to England to seek benefices. Gilbert Burnet was ordained in February 1665 by the Bishop of Edinburgh and became Minister of Saltoun in that year. In 1673 he retired permanently to England, where he became chaplain to Charles II for a short period. He received no benefice during the reigns of Charles II and his brother. However, in 1689 he was nominated to the see of Salisbury by William III and was consecrated on 31 March 1689.

In 1681 a number of Scottish clergy refused to subscribe to the Test Act and were deprived. Burnet wrote that their number was approximately eighty, and went on to add that

> . . . about twenty of them came up to England: I found them men of excellent tempers, pious and learned, and I esteemed it no small happiness that I had then so much credit, by the ill opinion they had of me at court, that by this means I got most of them to be well settled in England; where they have behaved themselves . . . worthily.[1]

One of those who came to England at this time was James Blair. He had been ordained on some date between 19 June and 11 July 1679, probably by the Bishop of Edinburgh, and had been Minister of Cranstoun, near Edinburgh, prior to his deprivation. Upon his retirement to England, he worked for three years in London. Bishop Compton was favourably impressed with this young Scotsman and sent him to Virginia as a missionary. He was successively rector of Varina Parish (later known as Henrico Parish), Jamestown Parish, and Bruton Parish. The question of his ordination was actually raised by some of his opponents in 1718 (especially by the Reverend Hugh Jones, professor at the Royal College of William and Mary, of which Blair was President), but it was his Scottish ordination which was in doubt. There was no suggestion that he had also received English ordination.[2]

---

[1] *History*, II, 318.

[2] Some research on this subject has been done by Edgard Legare Pennington, Miss Mary F. Goodwin, and George Maclaren Brydon. Blair was probably ordained by Alexander Young, who was Bishop of Edinburgh in 1673. In 1684 Blair received a certificate from John Paterson (not John Wishart, as in Brydon, pp. 275–6). The certificate stated that " . . . Mr. Jas. Blair, Presbyter, did officiate in Cranston, in my diocese of Edinburgh for several years preceding the year 1682". (Quoted in Brydon, pp. 275–6.)

Both Pennington and Brydon seem to believe that men were ordained in Scotland at this time either by a bishop or by presbytery. Brydon writes: "It may be inferred that congregations decided for themselves whether they would use the Prayer Book or have a nonliturgical service; and ministers might be ordained by a presbytery or by a bishop using the Anglican form" (p. 222). As has already been seen, all the evidence indicates that clergy of the Church

After the Revolution a number of ministers in Scotland were deprived, and some came to England, where they received benefices. James Gordon, son of the famous author of *The Reformed Bishop*,[1] was ordained by the Bishop of Aberdeen in 1686 "with the concurrence of some other ecclesiastick persons".[2] Although he continued to minister in Scotland for some years after the Revolution, he was eventually silenced by the Presbytery of Aberdeen, and he resolved in April 1702 to go to England. He recorded in his diary some of the preparations necessary for the journey:

> On the 28 and 29 [of April] I made a journey to & from Newtyle qr the Bp of Abd lived [George Haliburton, who lived at Newtyle in the Presbytery of Meigle after his deprivation] that I might procure Lers of ordination which I had not yet extracted because I was not actually going abroad, and in this matter I met with a very singular step of Divine Providence, for if I had lingred an hour longer than the precise tyme in qch I waited upon the Bishop the Episcopall seall had been sent off for Ireland at the earnest request of one who was to get some setlment thr but found himselfe at great loss for want of the Bps seall at his act of ordinaon altho it was signed by the Bp. so that if I had come but alitle later I had lost my design.[3]

The custom seems to have been that Scottish clergy who were going to England or Ireland took their letters of ordination with them. If these letters were in good order (but not otherwise), such men were accepted as having received episcopal ordination and were not reordained. This is precisely what happened to John Gordon when he reached England. He purchased a "Churchman's Habit" and had conferences with the Bishop of London,

of Scotland received only episcopal ordination during the Restoration period. (See above, p. 96.)

Blair was accused by the Reverend Hugh Jones of having received only presbyterian ordination because his certificate from the Bishop of Edinburgh did not state that Blair was ordained. The issue was whether Blair had received episcopal ordination in Scotland. He neither claimed (nor was he expected to have) orders from an English bishop.

See Pennington, *Commissary Blair*; Goodwin, *The Colonial Church in Virginia*, p. 251; G. M. Brydon, *Virginia's Mother Church*, I, 275–7; *Fasti*, I, 310.

[1] See above, p. 134.   [2] *Gordon's Diary*, p. 1.   [3] Ibid., p. 109.

M

who was "willing enough to doe for me but could not tell qn the occasion would offer". He read prayers in Rood Lane Church and baptized several children, at first using the Scots form and later the English. After about a year he received the living of Hawnby in Yorkshire, but before his departure to the north he "preached in S. Fosters and administrated the Sacrament (it being ther celebrated every sunday) & was well assisted". He received a small grant from the S.P.G. to assist in the journey of his family from Scotland to England, and he retained his living at Hawnby until his death in 1732.[1]

In all these cases, no evidence has been discovered to indicate that any of the men were reordained by English bishops. Many men who were deprived in Scotland went to England, and some were fortunate enough to receive benefices there. The orders of such men were accepted as valid when properly attested letters of ordination from a Scottish bishop could be produced.[2]

To what extent was there actual intercommunion between these two Churches? Or more accurately, was there in the Restoration period anything similar to what is now termed "intercommunion" between the Church of England and the Church of Scotland? It has been common for some historians to claim that nothing hindered complete intercommunion at this time. Thus

---

[1] *Gordon's Diary*, pp. 110–12, 121, 122, 2.

[2] Several other clergymen had a similar history. John Makmath became Minister of Ratho (Presbytery of Dalkeith) in 1633. Deprived in 1689, he went to England, where he became vicar of Grays Thurrock, Essex, on 5 October 1692. (*Fasti*, I, 329–30.)

John MacQueen was ordained in 1666 and became Sub-Dean of the Chapel Royal in 1688. He was deprived in 1689, and went to England, where he received the living of Welton, near Daventry, in Northamptonshire. (*Fasti*, I, 132.)

John Cockburn was Minister of Udny in 1676, was deprived in 1689, and in 1714 (after spending some time on the Continent) became rector of Northolt, Middlesex. (*Fasti*, I, 340–41.) In none of these cases is there any evidence of reordination.

Some of the men who came from Scotland were not quite so fortunate as to get a benefice. Alexander Malcolm became Minister of Orwell (Presbytery of Edinburgh) in 1663, and was deprived in 1689. In 1691 he went to England, but was advised by Bishop Burnet "to return and submit to the Presbyterian establishment". What became of him is unknown. (*Fasti*, I, 135.)

Mr Mechie writes: "Once again [after the Restoration] . . . we find the Church of England and the Church of Scotland in full communion for nearly thirty years. . . ."[1] Yet only at one point is there positive evidence of intercommunion—namely in the willingness of English bishops to accept the orders of men who had been ordained by Scottish bishops. No data have been discovered which indicate whether Englishmen made their communions in Scotland. The Eucharist was celebrated on such rare occasions that there would have been little opportunity to do so. Morer's very brief description of a celebration of the Lord's Supper suggests that he never actually saw such a service.[2]

There seems, then, to have been a friendly but undefined relationship between the two Churches. The English bishops made no attempt to consider in a formal way their relationship with the Scottish Church, apart from recognizing the validity of Scottish ordinations. Beyond that, the nature and extent of "intercommunion" cannot be defined precisely. Yet even the undefined and imprecise terms which the bishops did use reveals that they believed the relationship between the two Churches fell short of what they thought it should be, and that they were conscious of real differences which were barriers to that "mutual affection and communion" which they hoped to establish.

[1] Mechie, "Episcopacy in Post Reformation Scotland", *Scottish Journal of Theology*, 1955.
[2] *Short Account*, p. 62.

8

CONCLUSIONS ABOUT THE KIRK

THE Church of Scotland after the Restoration continued as
one Church. Although there were various parties within the
Establishment, it is fallacious to speak as if there were an Episcopal Church and a Presbyterian Church, or an Episcopal clergy
differentiated from a Presbyterian clergy. Two-thirds of the parish
ministers of the Church continued their pastoral duties within the
Establishment after the Restoration. Both before and after the
"restitution of the ancient government of the church by archbishops
and bishops",[1] the Church continued to exist as a single entity,
including within its life a large majority of the people of Scotland.

While this formal unity of the Church is obvious, was the
Establishment inwardly one Church? To what extent was there
a real marriage between episcopacy and presbyterianism? Many
historians have concluded that episcopacy was merely an instrument of royal control arbitrarily inflicted on a presbyterian
system. Thus G. D. Henderson quotes W. L. Mathieson with
approval: "Episcopacy in Scotland has never been more than a
government superimposed for political purposes on a Presbyterian Church." [2] The strength of royal control over the Church
of Scotland is undeniable, yet the bishops were clearly more than
mere political agents of the Government. The "Right Reverend
Father in God" [3] exercised real pastoral care for the people of
his diocese, and the presbytery and synod records show that the
lower clergy looked upon the bishop as one who had definite
spiritual responsibilities within the Church. Episcopacy and presbyterianism did not exist in, so to speak, watertight compartments.

[1] *Source Book of Scottish History*, III, 157.
[2] G. D. Henderson, *The Claims of the Church of Scotland*, p. 92.
[3] *Inverness and Dingwall*, p. 316.

Parish life was least affected by the restoration of episcopacy. Very occasional visitations by the bishop and presbytery, preaching tours by a bishop into some of the parishes, and a few (albeit important) local administrative problems which were referred to the Ordinary were the chief ways in which the episcopal office and authority were known. The few changes in parish worship were also identified with the introduction of episcopacy. After the Revolution the "changes" were suppressed and eliminated from the worship of the Established Church for many decades. The life and work of a presbytery were more intimately affected by the existence of the Lord Bishop. We have already traced in detail the numerous occasions on which there was a conjunction of episcopal and presbyterial authority and administration.[1] The greatest change occurred at the top. The suspension of General Assembly gave to the bishop and synod the major voice in the internal affairs of the Church. The bishop had an absolute veto on acts of synod, although all positive legislation was enacted by "the bishop with consent of the brethren of synod".[2]

But something more than an administrative union seems to have been achieved in certain other areas. Episcopal responsibility for the inner life and discipline of the Church underlies the bishop's supervision of examinations of candidates for ordination, his presence as the essential minister of ordination itself, his jurisdiction over the discipline of the parish clergy, and his exclusive right to impose excommunication. In each of these duties the bishop was expected to be more than an administrator and to exercise his responsibility as a Father in God to the clergy and laity of his diocese. That complete integration of episcopacy and presbyterianism was not achieved is obvious, but there was a greater synthesis of these two forms of polity in the Church of Scotland than has sometimes been recognized.

Nor was episcopacy merely an alien imposition upon the Church of Scotland, for there was considerable support for episcopacy at the Restoration.[3] While perhaps a majority did not look upon

---

[1] See above, p. 45 ff.　　　[2] See above, p. 86.
[3] See above, p. 2 ff.

the "Act Abolishing Prelacy" in 1689 as repudiating an element essential to the life of the Church, this attitude was by no means universal,[1] and it was only with difficulty that the "Episcopal" clergy were ejected in some areas.[2]

The re-establishment of episcopacy did not alter in any significant way the long Scottish tradition of Calvinist theology, discipline, and worship. But the bishop worked within that system as its chief minister, fulfilling the functions of a spiritual leader and not merely those of a political agent.

A settlement which embraced both Calvinism and episcopacy has few parallels in post-Reformation history, but it was one that worked. A large majority of moderate Presbyterians accepted the settlement, and those who favoured episcopacy on principle were likewise comprehended within its boundaries. It should never be overlooked that the Church laboured under the burden of a royal absolutism which knew almost no limits, and that it contended with the vehement opposition of a small minority. Yet the Establishment continued to function surprisingly well and with remarkably few signs of inner conflict.

If we compare the Church of Scotland with the sister Church in the south, it is obvious that the former in no sense shared the Anglican tradition. Except for the fact that it derived its episcopal succession from the Church of England, the Church of Scotland was no more Anglican than was the Church of Sweden. The worship of the Church in the north was moulded by no prayer book; a Calvinist disciplinary system administered by appropriate courts continued to flourish; there was no code of canons; a two-fold ministry of bishops and ministers sufficed, with no differentiation between those clergy who had received episcopal

---

[1] See, for example, the indignation with which the "Episcopal" author of *An Account of the Present Persecution* (1690) refuted the suggestion that there were none who supported episcopacy in Scotland (pp. 57f.). Episcopal sentiment seems to have been especially strong north of the Tay and among many of the nobility (Grub. III, 314ff.). While the exact strength of the two parties is a matter of debate, at least a strong minority continued to favour episcopacy.

[2] This was especially true in the north, where some of the "Episcopal" clergy continued to minister for years. James Gordon was not silenced until 1699. (*Gordon's Diary*, p. 2.)

ordination and those ordained by the presbyteries of the Church of the Covenants. Confirmation was not a part of Church life, and, save for the observance of Christmas and Easter, the pattern of the liturgical year was unknown. Those practices which had been so debated in England—i.e. kneeling, the cross in baptism, the ring in marriage, the use of the surplice—did not exist in Scotland and occasioned no controversy. Thus the restoration of episcopacy did not Anglicize the Church of Scotland. Although there were signs of interest in a closer approach to Anglicanism in a few quarters, such movements were small and tentative and had had almost no effect upon the character of the national Church. Indeed, a recognizable Anglicanism did not develop in Scotland until the eighteenth century.

The Restoration Church of Scotland may seem like a strange and incongruous fusion from the viewpoint of the twentieth century. Perhaps it would not have seemed quite so strange to John Knox or to some of the continental reformers.[1] But to those who are concerned with contemporary ecumenical endeavours, the Restoration Church is not without significance. That settlement would have little appeal today for those outside the Calvinist tradition. Yet it serves as an excellent example of the possibility of introducing episcopacy into the life of a Church, even of giving that order considerable authority, and of still retaining an ecclesiastical structure markedly different from that of Catholic tradition. Moreover, the Scottish Church can serve to remind us once again of the adaptability of the episcopal office and its capacity to function under the most varied of circumstances. For the Church of Scotland was a Church of "Bishop and Presbytery" where, for almost a generation, a successful union of Calvinist discipline and episcopal order was acceptable to the "generality of the people".[2]

---

[1] See Jacques Pannier, *Calvin et l'épiscopat*, Paris, 1927.
[2] *Source Book of Scottish History*, III, 205.

BIBLIOGRAPHY

Acts of the Parliament of Scotland, 1593–1707, vols. IV–XII, edited by T. Thomson and C. Innes. 1814–1875.

An Account of the Present Persecution of the Church in Scotland in several Letters. London, 1690.

Anglican Orders (English): The Bull of His Holiness Leo XIII and the Answer of the Archbishops of England. London, 1948.

Annals of Banff, compiled by William Cramond, vol. II. New Spalding Club, Aberdeen, 1893.

Brief and True Account of the Sufferings of the Church of Scotland Occasioned by the Episcopalians Since the Year 1660. London, 1690.

Brodie, Alexander, and James Brodie, *Diaries of the Lairds of Brodie.* Spalding Club, Aberdeen, 1863.

Brydon, George Maclaren, *Virginia's Mother Church*, vols. I–II, Richmond, Virginia, 1948.

Burnet, Gilbert, *History of My Own Time*, vols. I–II. Oxford, 1897.

Butler, D., *The Life and Letters of Robert Leighton.* London, 1903.

Chambers, Robert, *Domestic Annals of Scotland from the Reformation to the Revolution*, vol. II. Edinburgh, 1859.

Clarke, T. E. S. and H. C. Foxcroft, *A Life of Gilbert Burnet.* Cambridge, 1907.

Clarke, William Nelson, *A Collection of Letters addressed by Prelates and Individuals of High Rank in Scotland to Sancroft, Archbishop of Canterbury.* Edinburgh, 1848.

Confessions of Faith of Public Authority in the Church of Scotland. Glasgow, 1771.

Cowan, William, "The Scottish Reformation Psalmody", *Records of the Scottish Church History Society*, vol. I, p. 29, 1926.

Cunningham, William, *Diary and General Expenditure Book.* Scottish History Society, Edinburgh, 1887.

Daiches, Salis, "The Jew in Scotland", *Records of the Scottish Church History Society*, vol. III, p. 196, 1929.

Directory for the Publike Worship of God Throughout the three Kingdoms of Scotland, England and Ireland, Evan Tyler, Edinburgh, 1645. Reprinted in *The Book of Common Order and the Directory*, edited by George W. Sprott and Thomas Leishman, Edinburgh, 1868.

Donaldson, Gordon, *The Making of the Scottish Prayer Book of 1637.* Edinburgh, 1954.

Donaldson, Gordon, "Scottish Ordinations in the Restoration Period", *Scottish Historical Review*, October 1954.

Fasti Academiae Mariscallanae, edited by Peter John Anderson, vol. I.
New Spalding Club, Aberdeen, 1889.

Fraser, James, *Chronicles of the Frasers 916–1674*, edited by William
MacKay. Scottish History Society, Edinburgh, 1905.

Goldie, F., *A Short History of the Episcopal Church in Scotland*. London,
1951.

Goodwin, Edward Lewis, *The Colonial Church in Virginia*. Milwaukee,
1927.

Gordon, James, *Diary 1692–1710*, edited by G. D. Henderson and H. H.
Porter. Third Spalding Club, Aberdeen 1949.

Grub, George, *An Ecclesiastical History of Scotland*, vol. III. Edinburgh,
1861.

Henderson, G. D., *The Claims of the Church of Scotland*. London, 1951.

Henderson, G. D., *Religious Life in Seventeenth-Century Scotland*. Cambridge, 1937.

Hunter, A. Mitchell, "The Celebration of Communion in Scotland
since the Reformation", *Records of the Scottish Church History Society*,
vol. III, 1929, p. 161; vol. IV, 1932, p. 48.

Hunter, John, *The Diocese and Presbytery of Dunkeld, 1660–1689*, vols.
I–II. London.

Inglis, John A., "A Seventeenth-Century Bishop: James Atkine,
Bishop of Galloway 1680–1687", *Scottish Historical Review*, vol. XII,
January 1915, p. 135.

Keith, Robert, *An Historical Catalogue of the Scottish Bishops*. Edinburgh,
1824.

Knight, G. S. Frank, "The Bible in Scotland after the Reformation",
Records of the Scottish Church History Society, vol. V, 1935, p. 214.

Knox, E. A., *Robert Leighton, Archbishop of Glasgow*. London, 1930.

Lauderdale Papers, vols. I–III, edited by Osmund Airy. Camden Society,
1884.

Leighton, Robert, *Works*, vols. I–VI, edited by G. Jerment. R. Ogle,
London, 1805.

Leishman, Thomas, *The Westminster Directory*, London, 1901.

Le Neve, John, *Fasti Ecclesiae Anglicanae*. London, 1716.

*Letters, Illustrative of Public Affairs in Scotland addressed by Contemporary
Statesmen to George, Earl of Aberdeen, Lord High Chancellor of Scotland,
1681–1684*. Spalding Club, Aberdeen, 1851.

Lowndes, Arthur, *Vindication of Anglican Orders*, vols. I–II. New York,
1911.

Lyon, C. J., *History of St Andrews*, vols. I–II. Edinburgh, 1843.

MacKenzie, Agnes Mure, *Rival Establishments in Scotland*. London,
1952.

MacKenzie, Sir George, *A Vindication of the government in Scotland during
the reign of King Charles II against Mis-Representations made in several
scandalous pamphlets*. 1691.

MacLean, Donald, "Roman Catholicism in Scotland in the Reign of Charles II", *Records of the Scottish Church History Society*, vol. III, 1929, p. 43.

McNeill, John T., *The History and Character of Calvinism*. New York, 1954.

Mechie, Stewart, "Episcopacy in Post-Reformation Scotland", *Scottish Journal of Theology*, vol. VIII, 1955, p. 20.

Meikle, James, "The Seventeenth-Century Presbytery of Meigle", *Records of the Scottish Church History Society*, vol. V, 1935, p. 144.

Memorials of the Family of Skene of Skene, edited by William Forbes Skene. New Spalding Club, Aberdeen, 1887.

Miscellany of the New Spalding Club, vol. I. Aberdeen, 1890.

Miscellany of the Scottish History Society, vols. I–III. Edinburgh, 1893, 1904, 1919.

Miscellany of the Wodrow Society, edited by David Laing, vol. I. Edinburgh, 1844.

M'Millan, William, "The Anglican Book of Common Prayer in the Church of Scotland", *Records of the Scottish Church History Society*, vol. IV, 1932, p. 138.

Morer, Thomas, *A Short Account of Scotland*. London, 1702.

Nicoll, John, *A Diary of Publick Transactions and other occurrences chiefly in Scotland*. Bannatyne Club, Edinburgh, 1836.

"Parish Records of Canisbay", *Scottish Record Society Publications*, December 1914, p. 15.

Paul, James Balfour, "The Post-Reformation Elder", *Scottish Historical Review*, vol. IX, 1912, p. 253.

Pennington, Edgar Legare, *Commissary Blair*. Hartford, 1936.

Presbyterian Inquisition; as it was lately practised against the Professors of the College of Edinburgh. London, 1691.

Psalmes of David in Meeter, with the prose wherevnto is added Prayers commonly vsed in the Kirke, Andro Hart, Edinburgh, 1611. This is reprinted in the *Book of Common Order and the Directory*, edited by George W. Sprott and Thomas Leishman; Edinburgh, 1868.

Quig, Gordon, "Montrose's Chaplain—George Wishart, Bishop of Edinburgh", *Records of the Scottish Church History Society*, vol. V, 1935, p. 40.

Rait, Robert S., *The Parliaments of Scotland*. Glasgow, 1924.

Records of Elgin—1234–1800, vol. II, compiled by William Cramond. New Spalding Club, Aberdeen, 1908.

Records of the Kirk Session, Presbytery and Synod of Aberdeen. Spalding Club, Aberdeen, 1846.

Records of the Meeting of the Exercise of Alford, edited by the Reverend Thomas Bell. New Spalding Club, Aberdeen, 1897.

Records of Old Aberdeen, vol. I, edited by Alexander MacDonald Munro. New Spalding Club, Aberdeen, 1899.

Records of Old Aberdeen, vol. II, edited by Alexander MacDonald Munro. New Spalding Club, Aberdeen, 1909.

Records of the Presbyteries of Inverness and Dingwall, edited by William Mackay. Scottish Historical Society, University Press, Edinburgh, 1896.

Rogers, Charles, *Social History of Scotland*, Grampian Club, Edinburgh, 1884.

Scot, Hew, *Fasti Ecclesiae Scoticanae*, vols. I–VIII, Edinburgh, 1915–28.

Scotch Diaries and Memoirs: 1550–1746, edited by J. G. Fyfe. Stirling.

Scougall, Henry, *Works*. Glasgow, 1830.

Seafield Correspondence, edited by James Grant. Scottish History Society, Edinburgh, 1912.

Skinner, John, *An Ecclesiastical History of Scotland*, vols. I–II, London, 1788.

Snow, W. G. Sinclair, *The Times, Life, and Thought of Patrick Forbes*. London, 1952.

Source Book of Scottish History, vols. II–III, edited by William Croft Dickinson and Gordon Donaldson. London, 1953–4.

Stephen, Thomas, *The History of the Church of Scotland*, vols. I–IV. London, 1844.

Stephen, Thomas, *The Life and Times of Archbishop Sharp*. London, 1839.

Sykes, Norman, *Old Priest and New Presbyter*. Cambridge, 1956.

Thomson, J. Maitland, *The Public Records of Scotland*. Glasgow, 1922.

Torrance, John, "The Quaker Movement in Scotland", *Records of the Scottish Church History Society*, vol. III, 1929, p. 31.

Wodrow, Robert, *The History of the Sufferings of the Church of Scotland*, vols. I–IV. Glasgow, 1835.

INDEX